THE COMING ULSTER REVIVAL.

Saving Northern Ireland & The West, For The Glory Of God & For The Craic

Jamie Bambrick World International Mega Ministries With Its Own Dedicated Publishing House

The Coming Ulster Revival
Copyright © James Bambrick 2022

Requests for information to be sent to: My Facebook page
Otherwise, just Google me and see where that takes you
Actually, I just got a website for this:. www.thecomingulsterrevival.com
– original, right? There'll be a contact form there.

ISBN 9798793160148

"International"* Trade Paperback Edition
(*Precisely one dude outside of N.I. might buy this)

All Scripture quotations except those noted otherwise are taken from the English Standard Version Copyright © 2012 by Crossway. All rights reserved.
To be honest, I don't know if this means I needed permission to quote it or not. I hope not. Don't sue me Crossway.

All rights reserved. If you use this without my express permission, signed with my own blood, I will track you down and do terrible, terrible things.
I won't actually. I lack the skills or budget for that kind of thing. Also that was a joke, not a threat. I'd probably be complimented. Unless you outsell me, in which case I would likely weep.

Most people start their books by acknowledging someone here, so I probably should too.

Thanks to my wife Dany, for suffering with me as I attempt to write a book for some reason, and also just generally for being a great wife.

My son Jack – you made me determined not to depart this world without at least trying to improve our little corner of it.

Lots of others.

Reader beware:
This book is aggressively Northern Irish. At least I hope it is. There's lots of in-jokes, colloquialisms and general carrying on. If you're not from Northern Ireland, much of this will go over your head. I'd offer an apology, but ultimately it's your fault for not living here.

Table of Contents

1
Are You Wise In The Head?
Or: A Brief Defence Of Spiritual Petrol Bombs

5
What's The Craic?
Or: What Revival Is, And Why It's Needed

33
Our Wee Country
Or: Why Northern Ireland Is Worth Salvaging

63
Boys A Dear
Or: The Current State Of The Northern Irish Church

91
Keep 'Er Lit
Or: The Legacy Of Past Irish Revivals

121
That'll Learn Ye
Or: A Strategy For Revival In Our Day

151
It'll Be Class
Or: Why Revival Is Guaranteed

181
For God And Ulster, Our Time Will Come
Or: A Vision For A Christian Province

209
Bibliography

PREFACE

ARE YOU WISE IN THE HEAD?

Or: A Brief Defence Of Spiritual Petrol Bombs

I don't know why anyone would bother writing a book that doesn't at least stir up some controversy. Boldly going into all the world and saying things that everyone wholeheartedly agrees with seems pointless, for starters, and secondly, it sounds like an absolute snooze. It's also profoundly unbiblical.

So before you begin reading, you should be aware that the intention behind this book to be a sort of loving poke in the eye. My son understands this concept perfectly; any time I'm having a doze and he would rather I was, say, running around the room, or playing shops, or throwing a ball, he'll sidle on up to me and climb up onto my chest. Now by this point, I'm normally awake, but either groggy enough to not have opened my eyes yet, or I'm keeping them shut as a pretence of still being asleep, hoping he'll change his mind at this final second. Inevitably he doesn't, instead carrying out his predetermined plan of sticking his thumbs firmly onto my closed eyelids, and squishing them simultaneously inwards and upwards to a fully open position. If the light being forced into my corneas doesn't wake me by this point, the pain usually will. He's twenty-four, by the way; he should really have stopped this by now. (He's not; he's three.)

That's pretty much what I want this book to do for you. To the best of my ability, I'm writing it with the same good intentions as my son has for me. But we are in a spiritual slumber, we need to wake up and see what's happening, and a tactless interruption seems perfectly necessary at this point. At least, I can't think of a better way to wake anyone up right now.

As such, this book is not written in the style of most Christian literature. The bestselling Christian books - of which this will not be one - are written with about as much spice as the recommended food list for people with Irritable Bowel Syndrome. Mashed potato comes to mind. Designed for mass appeal and minimal offence, their pleasant truisms and helpful-but-not-exactly-revolutionary content are totally fine, but unlikely to provide the jolt we need.

The Bible, on the other hand, is like the literary equivalent of Planet Spice's Lamb Vindaloo. It's full of fiery quips, biting sarcasm, and the kinds of ideas that topple empires. Actually, it has toppled a few empires, now that I think about it. It's the book that accuses people of noticing a fleck of sleep in someone else's eye but not the snooker cue sticking out of their own. It's the book that laughs at the most self-important spiritual elites for not eating fruit that has had a bluebottle fly somewhere near it, but happily letting a filthy carthorse wade through their soup. It's the book that tells legalists to cut off their boy bits. Yikes.

Of course, the Bible does this for a reason; namely that it's a bloomin' good way to make a point. Its aim is not merely to fill people's heads with some true ideas, but to crack off the ice from frozen hearts and fling people into self-sacrificial, almost reckless action for the glory of God. My aim in my book, though not remotely in the same category as Scripture, is roughly the same.

Now whereas the Bible manages to do this absolutely perfectly, its ridicule and its hyperbole being mixed with perfect love, my book obviously won't reach such faultlessness. I may overstep some boundaries here and there, I may lack some finesse, and maybe even some wisdom at times. And if I knew where those points were right now, I would adapt them. But then again, not being able to do something perfectly is no excuse for not attempting to do something the Bible clearly models, flawed though those efforts may be. I don't love perfectly either, I don't pray perfectly, I don't serve perfectly, but the fact that I don't do them perfectly is hardly justification for not giving them my best efforts. Likewise, every Christian has an obligation to speak with the same boldness, clarity and zing as the Bible does, even though we will inevitably falter at some point.

I could write a bland, tasteless book that makes the occasional person say, "Hmm, that's nice," but no more, or I could write a book that leaves you no choice but to either reject it or act. I went for the latter. At the very least it should make for a provocative read. If it is successful, it might actually make an impact. Who knows?

CHAPTER 1

What's The Craic?

Or: What Revival Is, And Why It's Needed

The church is only ever one generation away from extinction, which is why every generation needs a move of God.

Nice opening line, right? I put a fair bit of work into that one. Well, a few minutes, but that's pretty long for a single sentence. It's true though, and very relevant for where we are today in Northern Ireland. But let me defend it, and explain how it applies to us.

God's people are not some kind of massive legacy business that, should it hit a bad patch, could simply run on the finances and goodwill stored up in former good times for a few years until things turn around. Think of companies with massive financial reserves, the great tycoons of industry: BP oil, Toyota cars, Tayto crisps - we're not like that. Sure, organisationally there are major denominations that would have enough property and steady funds to survive for some time financially, but a financially viable organisation does not a church make. *The* Church - the capital-C-Church, the invisible Church - is the people of God, transformed by the power of the Spirit, brought from darkness into light through supernatural rebirth, having true faith in Christ which is a gift from God. The invisible Church is the whole mass of those who are truly followers of Jesus across the globe. It is not just some conglomerate with property, payrolls and pastors.

Of course, it's fine for people in the invisible Church to create organisations that have all those things - it's biblical even, and such organisations are considered parts of the 'visible church'. These often *can* carry on for a while without a move of God, but the invisible Church simply cannot, because every single member is brought into that Church by His divine power. At some point they experience a personal work of the Spirit that makes them a new creation who trusts Jesus for salvation, loves Him for saving them, and hates their sin that made such a salvation necessary, thus making them part of His Church. That's a move of God. By definition, therefore, if God decided to stop moving at all in anyone's heart, as soon as the last person in the previous generation who truly believed died, the invisible Church would cease to exist on earth. Fortunately, we can have total confidence from Scripture and history that such total extinction will not happen. God is always in the business of saving individuals, and even in the darkest times, He preserves a remnant, a 'seven thousand who have not bowed the knee to Baal'.[1] So in one sense, saying we always need a move of God because we're always close to extinction is just a generic truism that has no actual weight attached to it. 'Yeah of course, duh. And He will move, we won't go extinct, so chill your beans.'

But though the threat of total, absolute, utter extinction might not be hanging over us like some Damoclean sword, we are being genuinely threatened with a

---
[1] 1 Kings 19:18

different kind of extinction today, and one that requires a specific move of God in our time. We are facing what could be called 'functional extinction'. In the animal kingdom, functional extinction is when a species of animal either has no role in the wider ecosystem, and/or the population is so diminished that it cannot reproduce.[2] That sounds like us. Though there will always be individual believers in our land because God always moves to save in that way, the church could experience such major decline that we cease to have any meaningful impact on society. The invisible Church may not disappear, but it can become so small, so diminished and so marginalised in a nation that it may as well not exist.

There are a couple of reasons why God may permit this sort of decline. Firstly, even those who truly believe in Jesus can become prayerless, errant, accommodating of sin, or just so plain lazy about their task that they need to experience some challenge to their faith to shake them out of their slumber. They're still true believers though, they just need a bit of a kick up the behind, as we all do from time to time.

However, the second reason why God would allow such a decline, and which almost always goes hand in hand with the first one, is that with the visible churches - the congregations and denominations that you and I know the names of - can become compromised beyond repair. They can become textbook examples of the flavour-free salt Jesus warned about in Matthew 5, having no meaningful purpose for God or man, and subsequently collapse in both numbers and influence.

---

[2] https://psmag.com/environment/what-happens-when-an-animal-is-declared-functionally-extinct accessed 9th December 2021

It's entirely possible for such an organisation to abandon its original beliefs and be populated by people who have no true knowledge of Jesus, meaning such 'churches' have very little to do with the invisible Church in the eyes of God. Imagine if Tayto stopped selling salty snacks and instead produced, I dunno, used toilet brushes or something. Even if it called itself 'Tayto Crisps' for the entire time, had a giant picture of a humanoid hat-wearing crisp on the wrapper, and put them in crisp vending machines, the whole shebang, it still wouldn't be a crisp company. The same is true for a church that disposes of its essential DNA - it's not a church even if everyone calls it some church-sounding name, like, say, hypothetically, Oasis Church Waterloo, or something like that.* The world and Christ can think of nothing to do with such churches other than to spit them out. *(This may or may not be the name of progressive pastor Steve Chalke's church.*) **(Alright, it is.)[3]

Functional extinction, as I've described it, is when the invisible Church shrinks to near-unviable levels, often due to its own flaws and foibles, and the visible church compromises to the point of total uselessness. As I write this, such functional extinction is a clear and present danger.

Now before you accuse me of bleak pessimism and weak faith, I'll have you know that there is biblical precedent for such a cataclysmic demolition of God's people. What I've termed as 'functional extinction' happened repeatedly to the people of God in the book of Judges, where we are told that after the death of Joshua, *"there arose another generation after them who did not know*

---

[3] http://www.oasiswaterloo.org/im-new-here/ accessed 9th December 2021

the Lord" (Judges 2:10). It's not the case that absolutely every single person in that generation had abandoned worship of God, but that the nation as a general collective had turned their back on the Lord, neither seeking His favour nor obeying His commandments. The true believers - let's call them invisible Israel - were basically ineffective, and visible Israel was in open rebellion against God. Those who are aware of the pattern of the book of Judges will know that this happened repeatedly to the nation, that those generations who forgot God were then subjected to judgement through their enemies, and delivered by a 'judge' who would see the people turn back to God for a generation, before their own children once again forgot and rejected Him.

Functional extinction is also what Jesus threatened would happen to several of the churches in the book of Revelation. In the opening portion of that book, Jesus warns many of the compromised churches that, if they would not repent of their various sins and doctrinal errors, He would *'remove their lampstand'* (Rev 2:5), or *'war against them'* (2:16), or *'come like a thief in the night against them'* (3:3). Written to congregations like *'the church in Ephesus'* and *'the church in Pergamum'*, these warnings were given to the entire established church in a city or region. Just as in the book of Judges, it's not that Jesus was saying that there were no true believers in these churches. In fact, this was very clearly *not* His intent, as in these same letters Jesus commends the faithful remnants within these wider congregations. Jesus' warning here is against the visible church, alerting them of a pending a swift drop into obsolescence. There were so few true believers that God was getting ready to remove the visible churches from these cities.

All that to say, when I claim that the church is only one generation away from extinction, and apply it to us today, I'm not concerned that Northern Ireland won't have any individual believers at some point in the near future. Rather, I'm concerned that the visible church in our land is compromising, broad swathes of the invisible Church are snoozing, and both are sliding into sad irrelevance. Judging from our current trajectory, this slide looks less like a small, shallow-angled playpark slide for toddlers, and rather more like an enormous near-vertical Kamikaze waterslide from a great height, ending with a dramatic splash and soaked onlookers. Except, if I follow my own analogy correctly, I believe we drown at the bottom, or something like that. Huge bummer.

The move of God we need is one which addresses this emergency. God, who's always up to something, sometimes works to simply introduce a fresh expression of what He was doing in the preceding generation, or to highlight a new area of culture that the church needs to reach, or an area of mission to expand out into. Sometimes He brings moves of consolidation, of deepening, of imparting something to future generations, or of ensuring spiritual health. But the move Northern Ireland needs today is more akin to a set of fully-charged defibrillator paddles applied repeatedly to the pulseless chest of the body of Christ, which is currently lying on a gurney somewhere whilst a heart-monitor sends out a shrill unbroken beep in the background. Perhaps some CPR and mouth-to-mouth might come in handy too. There should also be a doctor demanding fifty cc's of something 'stat'.

That is, we do not just need the kind of move of God in the heart of some individuals, though personal salvation is the backbone of every move of God, and neither do we need some pleasant divine encouragement about our healthy state. We need a bucket of cold water; a jolt from the blue; an airhorn six inches from our face. We need a widespread move of God that impacts an entire church in an entire region. A move of God that dramatically changes people not just in singles and smatterings, but in stadiums. A move of God that shakes the church, saves the lost, transforms society and builds the platform for the next move He wants to bring in those coming after us. A move of God that not only prevents our functional extinction, but propels us in the exact opposite direction, where the church becomes a fully-living, Spirit-filled, gospel-advancing, truth-affirming army, a kind of weapons-grade super-salt and blinding nuclear-fission light to its day, its impact sending shockwaves around the world. A move that transports the church from societal irrelevance to the epicentre of culture. A move of God for a whole generation.

In short, we need a revival.

What is revival?

I want to share a quick story about my sister, if that's all right with you? I'd say it's alright with her, but if I'm honest, I haven't asked her. In my defence, I'm her older brother, and as such I feel like I have a sibling version of the 'divine right of kings', except that instead of having the right to rule over a nation, I have the right to tell stories at her expense. Furthermore, just in case you're worried, don't fear; she lives far enough away that I'm in no immediate physical danger. No authors were harmed in the making of this book.

My sister, let's call her Sophie, because that's her name, is what I would describe as a 'verbal chameleon'. You know what a chameleon is, right? Those lizards that change colour depending on their environment. If you put them in a blue box, they turn blue; put them in a red box they turn red; put them in a yellow box, they turn yellow. Well, she is a verbal one of those. That is, she is one of those people that if you put her in a room full of people with a different accent... you get the picture? Yep, she adopts that accent. Notice that I did not say that she tones down her Northern Irish slightly to be more easily understood, which is fairly normal. Nope, she full on starts talking in a completely different accent. And might I say, she does so with full gusto and no shame at all, no matter how badly her fumbled imitation may be, or how offended people are.

To be fair to her, she's not attempting to mock anyone; it's a simple mental glitch that, whilst attempting to be sympathetic and easily understood, she and many other people naturally default into when speaking to someone who sounds different. That does not mean it isn't hilariously silly.

For instance, I remember we used to go on these package holidays when we were kids, and there would often be a youth group of some sort. Being package deals, you would find that most people would fly from round the UK from various major airports, and as such, the majority of folks there would be English. Upon arrival, I would hear my sister within moments break out into the kind of full faux-Cockney accent that would make Dick Van Dyke proud, saying things like, *"Hoi, moi nayme's Sowfee, Oi'm frum Norvun Oirland."*

Naturally, as her bigger brother, and as I said, having a God-given right to mock such nonsense, my ears perked up. Obviously you've got to respect the commitment. I'm pretty sure I saw her walking around with a top-hat and monocle at one point, but she denies this. Still, it was, let's say, extreme.

One time, I remember bumping into her going round with a gaggle of tween English girls, and her saying, *"Vat's moi bruvva, Jaymee."* Everything within me wanted to respond, in a brash, Texan drawl, *"Well, howdee partner, sure is great to meet you, Yee-Haw,"* and fire some finger-guns into the air, *"Pew-pew."*

Fortunately for her, once you remove her from that environment, her accent does return to normal. She presently lives just outside Sydney, Australia - hence her inability to slap me for sharing the preceding factoid about her - and her accent from the start of a phonecall to the end of it is markedly different. If you happen to phone her whilst she's out and about, throwing shrimp on the barbie on Christmas Day or whatever silliness they do down there, she'll commence the conversation in a thick Australian twang, saying something like, *"G'day mayte, how aaaa ya?"* But by the end of it, she's back to talking like she's from Belfast, perhaps even with a little bit too much conviction, *"Alright nay, cheerio, see youse soon."*

Now what on earth has this got to do with revival? Apart from providing a light interlude, it actually provides a pretty good analogy. Firstly, the church's primary problem is our inescapable tendency to start imitating the world, and secondly, a revival is God rescuing the church out of this state and bringing it back to normal.

When it comes to mimicking the world, I'm not talking about music and style, though I don't think anyone would bother arguing that this doesn't also apply in those areas. But though singing 'Shine Jesus Shine' whilst everyone is listening to gangster rap is a cultural faux pas, it's relatively innocuous; where it gets dangerous is when we copy the ideological trends sweeping the globe. Looking over the history of the West, we find that society tends to experience quasi-religious revivals around certain ideas at fairly regular intervals. Whether it's Modernism, Marxism or Postmodernism, or any of the various subcategories in each, we see a radical embrace of certain ideas, a total rejection of other ones, and attempts to remodel society from top to bottom along those lines. At every one of those points, a significant number within the church have decided to remodel Christianity in line with the latest ideas-du-jour. It's always a disaster. Furthermore, just as with Christian music, we're always a bit late on the scene.

For instance, classic postmodernism was the darling movement in academia in the 1960s, and began to impact the culture in the 1980s-1990s. Ten years later in the early 2000s, the emergent church showed up on the scene, with Rob Bell and Brian McLaren attempting to bring Christianity to the cutting edge of the trend that had just passed. Christianity's desperate attempt to fit in failed miserably, and that movement died out long ago. More recently, the world has gone through a 'woke' stage, with theories about alleged marginalised groups being privy to certain insights about reality, group guilt for 'oppressor groups', and acronyms like, LGBT, BLM and CRT sweeping the globe.[4] Whilst these are still culturally dominant and spiritually dangerous ideologies, some in the world have finally started to tire of all this silliness, yet apparently the church has just now decided to adopt them as the focal point of its activity. Words like 'Anglicans', 'Relevant Magazine' and 'Christianity Today' casually drift through my mind as I say that for some reason. I heard one commentator say something to the effect of, *"You know that woke ideology is about to go out of fashion because the church is currently trying to become cool by embracing it."* He has a point. Imagine the most popular nightclub in town; as soon as the local reverends' society figures out that's where all the cool kids are at and decides to make it their hangout, it'll die out pretty fast. (Actually, that seems like a decent tactic for destroying unethical businesses. But I'm getting off track.)

Our simulations of these ideas don't actually work to further the popularity of Christianity, because those who love such concepts have no need of a Christian version of them. To quote King Of The Hill, *"You're not making Christianity better, you're just making Rock and Roll worse."*[5] I've already said that music isn't the real issue at stake here, but the point stands. People know our version is a watered-down attempt to copy whatever is fashionable.

Imagine that my sister thought that by imitating accents that she was easing the world around her into becoming more Northern Irish - that'd be insane, right?

---

[4] LGBT - Lesbian Gay Bisexual Transgender
BLM - Black Lives Matter
CRT - Critical Race Theory
[5] Reborn To Be Wild, *King Of The Hill*, Created by Greg Daniels Mike Judge, season 8 Episode 2

Well, that's what we think we're doing in the church; 'we're being missional', we're gradually increasing our influence on the world. In reality, our garbled mix of worldliness with 'Christian' spirituality fails to offer the benefits - perceived or real - of either. People know it's a fake accent, and they don't need it.

When I said earlier that this imitation is our primary problem, and that revival is God rescuing us from this state and bringing us back to normal, it may have come as a shock to some of you. Our natural assumption is that a revival is a period of unusual blessing on the church, where the tangibility of God's presence, the fruitfulness of evangelism and the holiness of God's people are raised to levels that are decidedly *abnormal*. So how can I say that revival is God bringing the church back to normal?

Well, it's because we have the wrong definition of normal church.

We assume that normal church is the average church life as we have personally experienced it. Or perhaps, it might be the average church life as those in our nation have experienced it, even if our personal experience is slightly better than that. That is, we think that the normal church life at its best looks like decent preaching, some good worship, the occasional salvation, and a vague impression of God's presence in our midst from time to time. Sure, this might be what is normal for us, but that is not normal church.

When I Googled the definition for 'normal' in the interest of making my point, the first result was this: *conforming to a standard; usual, typical, or expected.* If the technical meaning of normal is the standard which someone expects it to meet, then who is the One who sets the standards for the church? I can assure you it's not us with our everyday experiences. Rather, it's the One who designed and initiated the church.

To Northern-Irish-ify this a bit: a friend of our family is loosely descended from Thomas Andrews, the man who designed the Titanic. As the designer of the Titanic, Andrews would know best what normal operation of the Titanic should look like. Primarily - and I'm no nautical expert - but I imagine it should be floating on top of the water, and moving in the direction known as 'forwards' rather the one known as 'down'. The fact that the experience of those on the Titanic involved a collision with an iceberg, and the fact that, for the majority of the time since its creation, the Titanic has been lying in bits at the bottom of the ocean, does not mean that this is the normal state of the Titanic. The normal state is defined by the designer, who sets the expectations for how it should operate.

My claim that we need a move of God that makes the church fully alive, filled with the Spirit, holy in practice, powerful in preaching and transforming the world around it, was not describing anything other than God's expected, normal standard for the life of the church. Our average experience has nothing to do with it.

Whilst it might appear normal to us, it isn't normal to God. It's not His expected standard, it's not His norm; and He's the one who gets decide what the norm is. What we term revival is much less God sending us into an *abnormal* state, and rather more Him drawing us back into the *true normal* to which He has called us.

To borrow the credibility of people much smarter than myself, let me quote J.I Packer and D. Martyn Lloyd-Jones on the definition of revival. Packer describes revival as, *"the visitation of God which brings to life*

Christians who have been sleeping and restores a deep sense of God's near presence and holiness," and later says that the constant factors in revival are: an awareness of God's presence, responsiveness to God's word, sensitiveness (sic) to sin, liveliness in community, and fruitfulness in testimony.[6] Lloyd-Jones similarly delineates that revival, *"... is in a sense a repetition of the day of Pentecost... The Spirit of God has descended into their midst, God has come down and is amongst them. A baptism, an outpouring, a visitation. And the effect of that is that they immediately become aware of His presence and of His power in a manner that they have never known before."*[7]

Sounds amazing lads, great work. Let me ask the rest of us though: which of those things are not supposed to be normal for the church? Should we not have God's presence? Are we not supposed to be lively in community? Is sensitivity to sin just for special occasions? Has the Spirit not already come down? Revival might feel unusual compared to our daily experience, but that's like a dry riverbed - made so because someone built a dam upstream - finding the refreshing rush of water unusual once the levee finally breaks. Revival brings the church back to its natural condition.

If we look at the great OT revivals, whether under the leadership of Samuel, Hezekiah or Josiah, we see the following basic pattern that exemplifies my point. Firstly, God had outlined in His law the requirements He placed on His people, the blessings for obedience, and the punishment for disobedience. The normal state, the expected standard for God's people, was that of

---

[6] https://bible.org/illustration/visitation-god accessed 9th December 2021 and further Gordon Pettie, *Do It Again Lord* (Fines Creek Publishing, 2017) page 7
[7] http://articles.ochristian.com/article1651.shtml accessed 9th December 2021

obedience and blessing. But then, in the time leading up to these revival movements, the people had drifted into compromise, idolatry and sin, either neglecting or outright rejecting God's word, living instead according to their own desires. Naturally this led to the waning of the nation, not merely spiritually, but economically and territorially. So, God sent bold leaders into such a climate, who upheld the law of God as their ultimate standard and called the people back to obedience. When they did, they were blessed as a result.

This was the role of the prophets; in Samuel's case, the national leader was also a prophet of God, and in the cases of Hezekiah and Josiah, the leaders worked hand in hand with such prophets to apply God's word to the sins and issues of their day. We often think of prophets as bringing new revelation, which to some extent they did, their words rightly being included in the canon of Scripture as the very words of God. But if you read them carefully, what you find is that they overwhelmingly harkened back to the word given to Moses on Sinai, the original expected standard for God's people. Sure, they added new layers of understanding, included specific future revelation, and gave fresh application of the law of God, all of it divinely inspired - but they never once added a new law. Their primary purpose was to bring the people back to God's norm.

Similarly, if we think about the great moves of God throughout church history, the emphasis has always been on a return to Scriptural faithfulness. The Reformation, for instance, came at a time when the church had fallen into the sort of rank legalism decried by Jesus and Paul when they confronted the Pharisees and Judaizers. In the midst of this corrupt, abnormal church life, God sent men like Luther, Calvin, Bucer and

Zwingli, not to call the church into some brand-new revelation, but to the rediscovery of an old one. Likewise the Methodist movement in Britain, and its transatlantic counterpart revival known as the Great Awakening, both called people to a return to the Scriptural concepts of rebirth, being born again, by the work of the Spirit, as opposed to a dead, philosophical 'faith'.

We see in both Scripture and history that God's people are never called to develop artificially manufactured jewellery, but to dig up buried treasure. Indeed, when someone comes along saying they have a new revelation from God outside of Scripture, they almost always turn out to be a blatant heretic. The Pharisees did this, adding their own 'Oral Law' to the words of God, and thereby both perverting and breaking the original commandments given to Israel.[8] Joseph Smith, the founder of Mormonism, or Mary Baker Eddy, the founder of Christian Science (which, I might add, is neither Christian nor science) could both fit under the heading 'Brand New Revelation Which Is Actually Just Old Heresy' perfectly.[9] Every true move of God, whether it be a great national revival, a world-sweeping reformation, or even a time of refreshing in a local congregation, is always centred on bringing God's people back to His normal.

The conditions for revival

I confidently believe we may be on the verge of such a revival in Northern Ireland.

---

[8] For a detailed analysis, read *Rabbinic Judaism Debunked: Debunking the myth of Rabbinic Oral Law* by Eitan Bar and Golan Brosh (One For Israel Ministry, 2018)
The Sermon on the Mount (Matthew 5-7) and Jesus' other interactions with Pharisaical teaching make this abundantly clear
[9] See details for these in Walter Martin's excellent work, *The Kingdom Of The Cults* (Bethany House Publishers, 2019 edition) pages 217-302 and 166-216 respectively

Of course, the first question you're probably asking yourself is, "Why on earth would you think that?" And I understand the question; things are hardly spiritually positive in our nation right now. In fact, later in this book I'll take a full couple of chapters to outline just how much trouble we're in. But I'll give you the short version right here: it's bad.

Fortunately, whether you look in Scripture or in church history, you find that revival always and only happens when things are bad. Indeed it's the fact that things are bad that makes revival necessary. Of course I certainly don't wish to make light of how desperate things are, or suggest that some sort of passive que-sera-sera, hakuna-matata optimism is anything like the kind of solution we need. Seriously, if we don't get our act together, we're in for a horrid couple of centuries in the Western world. But nonetheless, bad times are an excellent sign that revival is on the way at some point in the future. The question is: will it be in our day, or will we have to wait until our great-great-great grandchildren decide to do what we should have done, and allow all the generations in between to experience the darkness and evil that will be unleashed in the interim?

Few biblical examples of this surpass the great Old Testament revival under king Josiah. 2 Chronicles 34 outlines a move of God that was quite simply stunning, shaking the nation of Judah and dragging it back from the brink of destruction to arguably the most spiritually fervent it had ever been. We're told the following:

> *"Josiah was eight years old when he began to reign, and he reigned thirty-one years in Jerusalem. And he did what was right in the eyes of the Lord, and walked in the ways of*

David his father; and he did not turn aside to the right hand or to the left. For in the eighth year of his reign, while he was yet a boy, he began to seek the God of David his father, and in the twelfth year he began to purge Judah and Jerusalem of the high places, the Asherim, and the carved and the metal images. And they chopped down the altars of the Baals in his presence, and he cut down the incense altars that stood above them. And he broke in pieces the Asherim and the carved and the metal images, and he made dust of them and scattered it over the graves of those who had sacrificed to them."

(2 Chron 34:1-5)

So the young king, at the age of sixteen, begins seeking God, and at the age of twenty goes to war with the idols in his nation. Next, he commissions repair work on the temple. It had been lying in a state of neglect; and whilst the workers are analysing the now-derelict building, they come across some old scrolls, which turn out to be the long-lost Old Testament law.

"Then Shaphan the secretary told the king, 'Hilkiah the priest has given me a book." And Shaphan read from it before the king. And when the king heard the words of the Law, he tore his clothes."

(2 Chron 34:18-19)

It's only now that Josiah, having likely been guided thus far by a mixture of his conscience and second-hand reports of what God's law allegedly said, hears the word of God directly. He recognises just how deep the sin of the nation has been, how far they have fallen, and cries out in personal repentance before God.

The next step he takes is to widen that repentance from himself to the whole nation. He leads the people in a season of full-on contrite remorse for sin and a wholehearted renewal of their commitment to God. You can see just how sincere and thorough this was by simply noticing the number of times the word *'all'* is mentioned in the following passage:

> *"And the king stood in his place and made a covenant before the Lord, to walk after the Lord and to keep his commandments and his testimonies and his statutes, with **all** his heart and **all** his soul, to perform the words of the covenant that were written in this book. Then he made **all** who were present in Jerusalem and in Benjamin join in it. And the inhabitants of Jerusalem did according to the covenant of God, the God of their fathers. And Josiah took away **all** the abominations from **all** the territory that belonged to the people of Israel and made **all** who were present in Israel serve the Lord their God. **All** his days they did not turn away from following the Lord, the God of their fathers."*
>
> (2 Chron 34:31-33 - emphasis mine)

All the nation joins, and removes *all* the idols, from *all* of their land, and *all* served God, for *all* of Josiah's days, whilst he himself followed God with *all* his heart and *all* his soul. This righteous fervour culminates in the following chapter, where the nation throws a massive Passover festival, about which we are told:

"No Passover like it had been kept in Israel since the days of Samuel the prophet. None of the kings of Israel had kept such a Passover as was kept by Josiah, and the priests and the Levites, and all Judah and Israel who were present, and the inhabitants of Jerusalem."

(2 Chron 35:18)

It was the greatest celebration of God in the history of Judah, and an entire generation was saved. As I said, this was a truly stunning revival.

What makes it even more stunning is the context of the nation when Josiah arrived on the scene. If Josiah's reign was the high watermark of national repentance and holiness, the preceding generations were a similar high watermark of nationwide wickedness and idolatry.

For those who don't know much about biblical history, in the time of Solomon's son Rehoboam, around three-hundred years prior to Josiah, the one nation of Israel which consisted of all twelve tribes was divided in two across the middle. The northern kingdom was called Israel (which is rather confusing as the whole kingdom had been called Israel until that point) and the southern kingdom was called Judah. The northern kingdom decided to jump straight into idolatry, had pretty much only evil kings, and was carried off into exile in Assyria around two-hundred years after the division - eighty years prior to Josiah. The southern kingdom, where Josiah later reigned, was more mixed. They had some good kings and they had some bad ones; seasons of idolatry, and seasons of repentance; times of blessing and times of judgement. As a result, they lasted much longer before they were ultimately exiled in Babylon for a time, around twenty-five years after Josiah's death.

Of all the bad kings in the southern kingdom, the worst were Josiah's father and grandfather, Amon and Manasseh. These guys took the biscuit - the very malevolent biscuit, probably something foul like a Pink Wafer that's been left out of its packet for a good couple of weeks.

Manasseh began reigning as a twelve-year-old, and made it his personal business to offend God as quickly and as thoroughly as possible. He embarked on a national infrastructure project that involved not so much building roads as building altars to Baal and Asheroth, the bloodthirsty gods of the Canaanites. Then he went about 'altaring' the temple; that is, putting up altars to these false deities in the house of God, not merely in the outer court, but in the even-holier inner court as well. Deciding this was not enough, he carved an idol statue and put it alongside those altars in God's house. Not stopping there, he engaged in all sorts of demonic practices, from fortune-telling, to sorcery, to using mediums and necromancers. And just in case you thought, *"Well he might have worshipped the wrong gods, but he was probably a nice guy deep down,"* he topped it off by shedding enough innocent blood to fill Jerusalem from end to end, and burned his own sons as an offering to his idols.[10] So, erm, no, not a great guy or a great king.

Amazingly, when God judged the nation by sending the Assyrian army against the nation and they captured Manasseh, he actually repented of his sin and turned back to God. Though a wonderful story of personal salvation and how God both can and will forgive

---

[10] (See all of this in 2 Chron 33:1-18 and 2 Kings 21:1-18.)

anyone, the damage to the nation was untold. We're told of him that he led Judah *"to do more evil than the nations whom the Lord destroyed before the people of Israel,"* (2 Chron 33:9). Ultimately there was not enough time before his death for him to undo the idolatry which he had established in the nation.

We're not told a lot about Amon, Manasseh's son and Josiah's father, other than that he was worse. Sheesh. After describing Amon's personal commitment to idols, 2 Chron 33:23 says, *"And he did not humble himself before the Lord, as Manasseh his father had humbled himself, but this Amon incurred guilt more and more."* Whatever guilt Manasseh had, Amon added to it. Judging from what we just said about Manasseh, that must have been pretty bad. God allows him to be murdered by his own servants, a fitting ending for a murderous king.

At the end of all this, they had offended God at every turn for fifty years and two regimes, so that by the time of Josiah's coronation the nation was ripe for judgement. Indeed you could argue that this judgement had already begun. Isaiah 3, and verse four in particular, tells us that when children are installed as kings, that itself is a sign of God's wrath on the nation. Remember how Josiah took the throne aged eight? Even him being in power was a sign of God's profound anger at the condition of Judah.

Yet it was at this point, on what would seem to be the eve of destruction, that God sent the greatest move of the Spirit that the southern kingdom had ever witnessed.

That is always the case with revival: God sends it when we need it most. Whether on a personal or at a corporate level, God allows His people to be pushed to the brink, to stand on the precipice and look down into the abyss, before He delivers them. I'd say He's a daredevil, but applying any term with the word *'devil'* in it to God would be inappropriate. He's a daredeity.

This was not only true in Josiah's time, but all the other great moves of God in Israel. Prior to Samuel, the priesthood was corrupt and the nation under the thumb of the Philistines until God sent a prophet. Likewise in Hezekiah's day, it was not until Jerusalem was surrounded by a vast army, far beyond its strength, that God sent a rumour and a plague that send their enemies running. And it was true at the time of Christ, when the religious leadership was corrupt, Israel was subjugated by the Romans, and God had been silent for four-hundred years, when God finally sent the Messiah.

Furthermore, God doesn't just act like this in the Bible, He acts this way in history.

Arguably the greatest move of God in Britain was the Methodist revival, but if you look at the historical context, it was something no one would have predicted. In the early 1700s, just prior to this movement, the nation was in a deep spiritual quagmire. For starters, the church was a cesspit of compromise with the spirit of the age, Sir William Blackstone writing that, after visiting all the big-name churches in London, he *"did not hear a single discourse which had more Christianity in it than the writings of Cicero."*[11] And as a result of the church's weakness, the society around it was collapsing. Diane Severance summarises,

---

[11] https://www.christianity.com/church/church-history/timeline/1701-1800/evangelical-revival-in-england-11630228.html accessed 10th December 2021

> "*Drunkenness was rampant; gambling was so extensive that one historian described England as "one vast casino." Newborns were exposed in the streets; 97% of the infant poor in the workhouses died as children. Bear baiting and cockfighting were accepted sports, and tickets were sold to public executions as to a theater. The slave trade brought material gain to many while further degrading their souls. Bishop Berkeley wrote that morality and religion in Britain had collapsed "to a degree that was never known in any Christian country.""*[12]

Yet it was at this time that God sent the Wesleys and Whitefield to the highways, byways and fields, preaching to colliers and smithies in the open air, and seeing a revival that, if we adjusted for population growth, saw the equivalent of eight million converts in the UK. Nineteenth-century historian William Lecky convincingly argued that this movement saved Britain from a cross-Channel-equivalent to the insurgent atheism and subsequent mass bloodshed of the French Revolution. If you had asked in the late-1720s which was the more likely future of Britain, revival or revolution, there would only have been one answer - and not the good one. Like it or not, this seems to be God's modus operandi.

You might well ask, "Why exactly does God allow us to be pushed to such extremes before He moves? Why not do it earlier - pre-empt the disaster and cut it off before it gathers steam? Why does He always need to be lastminute.com?"

---

[12] Ibid.

Fair question. There are many places I could turn to in order to answer this question, and deep theological roots we could dig up in the process. But in the aim of succinctness, I believe the apostle Paul summarises the answer nicely when talking about his personal tribulations in 2 Corinthians:

> *"For we were so utterly burdened beyond our strength that we despaired of life itself. Indeed, we felt that we had received the sentence of death. But that was to make us rely not on ourselves but on God who raises the dead."*
>
> (2 Corinthians 5:8b-9)

Notice Paul's language: these trials happened to *'make them'* not rely on themselves. When things are going well, we have an inescapable tendency to rely on ourselves. *'Here's a great church strategy. Here's a new program to move things forwards. Here's how we can increase giving. Here's the best way we can think of to reach the lost.'* It's often connected to good activity, but if our trust is founded less on the power of God to save and more on our ability to strategise, there's a fundamental problem that God wants to resolve. Even Paul had to be forced, by divine providence and dire circumstance, into truly relying on God.

The tendency to trust in self is a natural fleshly wrinkle that needs to be ironed out of us by the steady, repeated pressure and heat of desperate crises. It's healthy for us to find ourselves in situations where God gets to be the only hope and the only hero. We need to see that we can't escape death, and yet be reminded that we know the One who raises the dead. Revival is not about great men, but a great God. He must get every last ounce of the glory.

All of which gives me enormous hope for Northern Ireland. Why? Because things look thoroughly hopeless right now. We'll take time later to look at just how bad the situation is, but all the stats, all the trends, and the large majority of churches paint the same depressing picture: a Jackson-Pollock-esque splattered mess of spiritual downturn. Functional extinction is waiting for us just around the corner, and we're moving at speed. I don't know if 'un-revival' is a word, but if it is, it describes our condition perfectly. Actually, now that I think of it, there is a word for un-revival: *death*. We're dead. Spiritually dead.

Brilliant. It's a perfect time for God to show up and bring us back to life.

Discussion Questions

1 – Have you noticed the need for revival in Northern Ireland, and if so, in what says have you noticed it?

2 – Have you felt urgent about pursuing a revival, or have you lost that urgency? What do you think you need to do differently to pursue revival?

3 – What have you considered normal church to be, and how does that differ from normal church in the Bible?

4 – If God has a pattern of moving when things look bleak, then what would you expect a move of God to look like in our day?

CHAPTER 2
OUR WEE COUNTRY
Or: Why Northern Ireland Is Worth Salvaging

Can I be honest with you? I never wanted to live in Northern Ireland. Growing up here, it just seemed so small, so pokey, so irrelevant, so detached from the wider world, that a future in Belfast was a million miles away from my youthful delusions of grandeur. People from other countries used to always come and talk about how pretty it was. Not to me. Cliffs, sheep, sea and drumlins felt much less interesting having grown up around them; if you've seen one green hill, you've seen them all, or so I thought. And the accent: gosh. I lived in Sweden for a few years (long story) and landing back in Belfast International I was confronted by a cacophony of harsh 'r's, guttural how-now-brown-cow sounds, and the general quasi-grumpy tone we use - a far-cry from the soft, melodic Swedish hurdy-gurdies. It just seemed like a wet, dull, miserable place where dreams went to die. Moving back here from Scandinavia did nothing to change my opinion. I'm pretty sure I made a quip one time about pulling the plug out and letting the island sink into the Atlantic.

Then we moved to England.

I quickly realised that Northern Ireland actually has quite a lot going for it that I had previously overlooked. Firstly, it's just the right size, not pokey at all actually, but just big enough to have a buzz without being so big that you feel inconsequential. The people may have seemed like they were detached from the wider world - but that's not it - they are attached to each other. Relevance is not defined here by glitz and glamour but actually mattering to the lives of real people around you. Oh, and the scenery! Behold the majesty of the sheer cliffs, the rolling hills dotted with white, fluffy sheep; the ever-present coastline where green meets blue. And the accent; how we sing! Every note like the melody of a flute or uilleann pipe (pick your synonym of choice depending on your background). We folks here say our 'r's properly, with gusto, like we mean them. Goodness, we even invent new ways to say fantastic words like how, now, brown and cow, just to be different. Heaven's angels spend their days learning to speak like us. Wet and miserable you say? Not a chance; 'refreshing' is the operative word. Life-giving rain soaks the ground daily, producing crops, watering the grass, and ensuring that even the ducks rejoice in God's favourite nation. It's a place of the Lord's most profound blessings at every turn, a land where dreamers are born. Let the world sink into the ocean, but let Northern Ireland remain - that's what I say.

So, it turns out I may not have thought much of living in England. Or rather, whilst England isn't a patch on Northern Ireland, it's much more the case that as soon as I left, I realised that God had put this nation in my heart. From a ministry perspective, I'd still love to do something that has an impact on the UK as a whole, but there's not a chance I'm doing it living anywhere other than here. Moving away was the very thing needed to uncover a hidden love for everything Ulster.

If we're aiming to have a revival in Northern Ireland, it seems like it would be worthwhile mentioning something about 'why here?' What makes this place worth reviving?

So what exactly is a 'Northern Ireland'?

I'll preface this section by saying that I'm not a sociologist, and I'm not trying to be one. It's possible that some nerd could come along with a peer-reviewed study and disagree with my assessment of Northern Irish culture, in which case, I'll defer to them and their geeky ways. However I imagine that most native readers will see that my analysis is relatively self-explanatory common sense.

It's often assumed that Northern Ireland has two cultures living side by side: Catholic and Protestant culture respectively. To some extent, this is evidently true.

The University of Minnesota defines culture as *"the symbols, language, beliefs, values, and artifacts that are part of any society."*[13] Certainly, when you go around Northern Ireland, you see two different sets of all of the above. Take symbols for instance: one half of the community likes to paint their kerbstones red, white and blue; the other half likes green, white and gold. One half has murals saying *'For God And Ulster'*; the other half prefers *'Eiri Amach Na Casa'*. And let's not get started on *flegs*. Or take language: the street signs in one half of the nation include both Gaelic and English, the other half has English only. Beliefs? Catholic, Protestant - no need to add anything. Values tend to be split, with Irish

---

[13] https://open.lib.umn.edu/sociology/chapter/3-2-the-elements-of-culture/ accessed 13th December 2021

nationalist and politically progressive on one side, and Unionist and politically conservative on the other. Artefacts such as St Paddy's Day and Irish dancing are celebrated by half of the nation, whereas the 12th of July and marching bands are celebrated by the other half.

So it's certainly not wrong to say that Northern Ireland has two cultures. Indeed, most Northern Irish people would wholeheartedly agree with such a sentiment, and know which side of the cultural divide they are on. I remember watching a news interview on the 11th July one year, where a reporter had cornered a couple of young teenage girls out getting ready for bonfire night. When he asked them why they were there, they said, *"Because it's our culture."* He then asked, *"And why do you burn the Irish flag on the bonfire?"* they quickly replied, *"Because that's not our culture."* Simple. The divide is pretty straightforward and it doesn't take a sociology degree, or even a single GCSE, to see it. (I'm not slagging the wee girls - they were too young to have done GCSEs - I'm just pointing out that it's a very obvious cultural split.)

However I would argue that the Catholic-Protestant divide in Northern Ireland is actually representative of two subcultures within the framework of a broader, unifying culture. Northern Irish Catholic culture and Protestant culture, rather than being totally incompatible, are more like two sides of the same cultural coin.

A truly different culture has values, artefacts, symbols and beliefs that are completely incoherent to outsiders unless they are explained. The Swedes, for instance, celebrate *Valborg,* an annual bonfire-based celebration that originated in honour of Saint Walpurga (class name!) and which almost no-one in Northern Ireland would either have heard of or recognise as significant. They have values such as *lagom:* a Goldilocks-style principle of everything being 'just-right'; they have norms like a daily routine called *fika*: a glorified coffee break; and they have a highly secularised, culturally left-wing belief system in their society. All of the above are fundamental to understanding their civilisation and are totally foreign to a true cultural outsider. A genuinely distinct culture is where the value of these things is not remotely understood by such outsiders unless they're explained.

The Northern Irish divide is not like that at all. Whilst the colour of kerbstones and the slogans on murals may provoke different reactions to different sides of the community, everyone understands exactly what they mean. One half of the country thinks something is a good thing, the other half thinks it's a bad thing; but we all agree it's a thing. A Northern Irish Catholic seeking to be warm and accommodating to a Northern Irish Protestant would instinctively understand the things that might cause a negative reaction, and tone them down. Likewise, should someone from one side of the community want to aggravate someone from the other side, they would be able to do so in a heartbeat. We are actually two poles on the same magnet, sharing a common understanding but with diametrically opposite reactions.

Despite the inevitable protest the following statement will doubtless receive, our shared culture means that today's Ulster Catholics have a far stronger cultural affinity with Ulster Protestants than they do with the Irish, and today's Ulster Protestants have a far stronger cultural affinity with Ulster Catholics than they do with the English. Let the wailing and gnashing of teeth commence. It's still true.

In the interest of not just leaving it there, I'll try and prove it. Maybe you don't agree; ok, look at it with me, and see if I can change your mind. If there is a common cultural superstructure, what does it consist of?

The first element, which perhaps will have been obvious from this chapter thus far, is that we have an overtly religious society. A compelling argument can be made that the Catholic-Protestant division was a cultural and ethnic divide rather than a religious one, with the violent elements on each side in particular rarely either practising a faith or believing any religious creed at all. The rubrics of Catholic and Protestant were, much more often than not, completely detached from true Catholicism or Protestantism. Bombings and shootings are certainly detached from the official teachings of either. Indeed, multiple popes and multiple Protestant church leaders explicitly and repeatedly condemned the violence. But gangs have to have some banner to fight under, I suppose.

That does not mean, however, that Northern Irish society is irreligious. Any eejit knows that's not the case. Religious observance in Ulster is much higher than most of the Western world. Around 80% of the Northern Irish population consider themselves Christian, compared to under 60% for England, Scotland and Wales - and whilst the remaining 20% of the population, those who consider themselves to have no religion, is a significant increase on the mere 7% of the population that made this claim in 2011, the total number of religious adherents is still extraordinarily high.[14]

---

[14] https://faithsurvey.co.uk/uk-christianity.html accessed 13th December 2021

Furthermore, religious practice is vastly beyond anything seen in the rest of the UK. 52% of professing Catholics attend mass regularly, and 43% of Protestants are also regular churchgoers.[15] Doing my own maths here - reader beware - that means that around 40% of the province consider themselves to be at least a somewhat regular church attender.

To put these numbers into a wider context, Catholics make up a much larger portion of the overall population in the Republic of Ireland - around 78% - but a mere 34% of them attend mass regularly.[16] That's over 15% lower than Northern Irish Catholics, in what was historically one of the most Catholic countries in the world. So, though Northern Ireland as a whole is much less Catholic than the Republic because half of us are Protestants, our Catholics are *way* more Catholic than theirs. I'm not the least bit Catholic, but if you're going to be one, at least do it properly.

Or we could look at it this way: the current Northern Irish 40% of the population in regular church attendance displays a significant contraction since the latter half of the 20th century, when around 80% of Catholics and 50% of Protestants were regular church attenders. But in the rest of the UK, church attendance currently sits at around 5% of the total population.[17] So, even after such a decline, we are still eight times as devout as the bunch of absolute pagans across the water. (I jest. Kind of.)

---

https://www.belfastlive.co.uk/news/belfast-news/20-ni-adults-now-consider-18445392 accessed 13th December 2021
[15] https://sluggerotoole.com/2018/07/01/doctrine-and-decline-irish-churches-and-the-conservative-turn/ accessed 13th December 2021
[16] https://www.cso.ie/en/releasesandpublications/ep/p-cp8iter/p8iter/p8rrc/ accessed 13th December 2021
https://sluggerotoole.com/2018/07/01/doctrine-and-decline-irish-churches-and-the-conservative-turn/ accessed 13th December 2021
[17] https://faithsurvey.co.uk/uk-christianity.html accessed 13th December e021

Though historically marked by nominalism, dead religiosity, and of course vulgar sectarianism, the fact remains that religion is a key component of Northern Irish culture. People are, on average, much more aware of religious stories, ideas and terminology, and at the very least claim to think along these lines. Furthermore, as the rest of the world chucks Christian ideals overboard like a dinghy-sailing-UDA-drug-smuggler disposing of evidence in Strangford Lough with the peelers in hot pursuit, today we find that believing Catholics and believing Protestants have much more in common with each other than they do with the rabid secularism found in the majority of the West.

As I said, I'm no Catholic; I so strongly disagree with many of the central dogmas espoused by the Vatican that I do not believe one can hold to them *consistently* (emphasis on this word) and be truly regenerate. * And I fully expect any knowledgable Catholic to think the same thing about me, because that is what Catholic teaching states. That's fine; I like them plenty anyway, and I want them to like me anyway. But despite our nigh-insurmountable theological divide, I am in many ways much closer to a devout Catholic than I am to a secularist. I don't just disagree with secularists on the doctrine of salvation, but also on theology proper, anthropology, and issues like sin and truth. I'm much closer to Catholics than secularists on all of the above. That includes secularists masquerading as 'liberal Protestants'.

When the surrounding world was more explicitly Christian, the differences between Protestantism and Catholicism were an important point of distinction, and therefore also of conflict. Today, now that the outside world has abandoned Christianity, Protestantism and Catholicism actually make us much more alike. Sectarianism is on the wane, whilst Christianity is still a key part of Northern Irish culture, whether one finds oneself on the Catholic side of the divide or the Protestant side. I'll argue to my dying day that historic Protestantism is true, but the common denominator of Christianity, errant or otherwise, is still so prevalent and so unique that it significantly separates us from the wider Western world.

(*Fortunately, because Protestantism is true, and because many Catholics are inconsistent with the teaching of their church, many professing Catholics can and will be saved by simple trust in Jesus alone. Such simple trust in Jesus alone for salvation is categorically denied as heresy by Catholicism, but thankfully accepted in reality by lots of Catholics.)

A second element of the common Northern Irish culture is a strong sense of the local. That is, most of the population lives in actual communities where people know each other, and the average person feels a genuine bond to their hometown or area.

Think about it: if you are Northern Irish (I imagine most of those reading this are) and you ask a fellow Northern Irishman where they are from, how do they reply? If they're from the countryside, they'll say something like: Ballycastle, Tandragee, Maghera or Kilkeel. Or if they're from Belfast, they'll say something like: The Cregagh Road, Andytown, The Falls, or The Shankill. They'll say this, fully expecting that you have at least heard of the place, and probably know roughly where it is. And most of the time, you will.

This is a unique mindset. Having lived in England and in Sweden, almost no one in either nation identifies themselves as 'coming from' somewhere as small or as precisely defined as we do. Comparatively few people have a strong attachment to 'coming from' anywhere at all actually; it's not a part of their identity in the slightest. The boundaries are more fluid, families are more spread out and people move around much more, and so a sense of 'being from' somewhere is an alien concept.

David Goodhart, in his book *The Road To Somewhere*, divides the world *"between the people who see the world from Anywhere and the people who see it from Somewhere."*[18] There are Anywhere people who see themselves as being portable, detached, flexible and part of a wider, global community, but are not really connected to a meaningful local community, and Somewhere people, who are rooted in their local setting, and think of themselves as Scottish farmers, working class Geordies, or Cornish housewives etc.

Well, Northern Ireland goes a lot further than that. Going well beyond Goodhart's definition of Somewheres, who define themselves by being from somewhere that is as 'local' as Scotland, we tend to define ourselves not merely by being Northern Irish, but define it down to exactly what part of Northern Ireland that is. We're not just Northern Irish, we're East Belfast Prods and West Belfast Catholics, we're from mid-Ulster and we're from the Ards Peninsula, we're Culchies and Derry Girls. And we're chuffin' proud of it, thank you very much. If the Western culture is now dominated by

---

[18] David Goodhart, *The Road to Somewhere: The Populist Revolt and the Future of Politics* (Penguin, 2017) page 3

Anywheres, Northern Irish culture is chock-full of Uber-Somewheres.

That includes many people like me. As I grew up, I fancied myself to be an Anywhere, but when I went to Anywhere, realised I was a Somewhere. I found out that my Somewhere had seeped into my bones, and that I loved my Somewhere, so I returned to my Somewhere, and now I plan to live and die in this Somewhere, because nowhere in the Anywhere compares. I'm not sure if that was all totally coherent, but it was heartfelt nonetheless.

Part of this local emphasis comes from the fact that Northern Ireland has a small population. By definition, this means that smaller settlements are comparatively more important because they make up a larger percentage of the total population. If it were situated in a state like California, with forty million inhabitants and megacities like Los Angeles, San Francisco, and San Diego, literally nobody would have heard of somewhere like Newry with its population of roughly 30,000.[19] It would be a backwater town with absolutely no name recognition at all. In Northern Ireland, it may still be a backwater town, but at least everyone has heard of it. (I know, it's technically a city, but seriously…) In fact, it's the 11th most populous locality in the province. Because of our small overall population, relatively smaller places develop a sense of importance, pride, and attachment that they would not otherwise have. I actually didn't look this up until I had already written the above passage, and so didn't choose Newry for this reason at all, but the town motto perfectly exemplifies the value of

---

[19] https://en.wikipedia.org/wiki/List_of_localities_in_Northern_Ireland_by_population accessed 13th December 2021

the local. It reads, *"Everyone's welcome, and no-one's a stranger."*[20]

It's not all positive, however, as this sense of the local also can be traced back to the Troubles. Violent times mean that people stay close, where they know their neighbours, the terrain and where they should and should not go at certain times of the day. During our thirty-year conflict, periods of increased bloodshed caused ever-more Catholics living in Protestant neighbourhoods to move out, and equivalent numbers of Protestants in Catholic neighbourhoods to do the same. You might think that periods of relative peace would encourage them to move back, but they never returned.[21] No one wants to be the first and only Catholic living in a Protestant area, or vice versa. The scars run deep; seen in postcodes and 'peace walls' (only necessary in times of war). Being local not only unites Northern Irish communities; it divides them.

But despite a chequered history, Northern Irish society still maintains many of the benefits of a local focus. Regardless of how local communities were built, and the downside they may entail in our context, built they have been and standing they remain today. The people of Ulster know their neighbours, invest in their areas, and make a difference in the lives of those around them. Our political system, as damaged as it is, at the very least shows that people care about the five streets either side of them much more than some distant Downing Street oligarchy. Sure, Stormont can get stuffed, but Westminster can get double-stuffed. However we

---

[20] https://www.belfasttelegraph.co.uk/imported/talking-shop-words-of-wisdom-for-newry-28092573.html accessed 13th December 2021
[21] Centre for the Study of Conflict School of History, Philosophy and Politics, Faculty of Humanities, University of Ulster, *Ethnic Residential Segregation in Belfast*, Paul Doherty and Michael A. Poole https://cain.ulster.ac.uk/csc/reports/apartbel.htm#conclude accessed 9th December 2021

arrived at it, for good or ill, Northern Irish culture has such a robust emphasis on being Somewheres that we stand apart from the shallow, rootless Anywhere-ism seen in most of the Western world.

There are many other aspects of Northern Irish culture that we could talk about at length if we had the time. For instance, our unusual levels of warmth and friendliness. My wife has a mobile hairdressing business where she travels to people's houses to cut their hair, and she often ends up doing haircuts for multiple kids or for elderly people. The hospitality, compassion and the kindness of people in Belfast, from all strata of society, is genuinely remarkable to her, and stands out when compared to doing the same role in other countries. She's constantly coming home with a wee cake some lovely auld dear has made for her, or laughing about the stories from a fellow mum. It's not just her, obviously; most visitors agree that Northern Ireland stands among the friendliest places in the world.

Or we could talk about our unflinching commitment to 'the banter'. It might sound like I'm being facetious here, but I'm not at all; engaging in banter is an absolutely essential part of the Northern Irish social fabric. What do you do when you meet someone new and want to make them feel comfortable? You rake the life out of them. Most cultures in the world would find it disrespectful to get on like this; in Northern Ireland, it's disrespectful not to. Banter is so integral to our relationships and interactions that if someone can't engage in it, they're often resigned to life as an outsider.

Those two features and many others like them, whilst important to understanding Northern Irish culture, may not have the same counter-cultural potency as either our religiosity or our emphasis on the local. One final element that likely does have that kind of impact, however, is that we still have much stronger family values than much of the West.

Now Northern Irish statistics on this area are not the easiest to track down - we don't put a lot of funding into tracking this data effectively. But the few that we do have bear out this fact. For instance, though marriage rates are on the wane, Northern Ireland still has roughly four-and-a-half weddings for every thousand people each year at present, well ahead of England and Wales, Belgium, the Netherlands, France, Spain and Italy.[22] In 2014, only 5% of couples cohabited before marriage in Northern Ireland, compared with 14% in the South of England. And the divorce rate is the lowest in the UK, with the average duration of marriages that end in divorce being sixteen years in Northern Ireland, compared to just eleven years in the rest of the UK.[23] There's a reasonable chance the hard numbers may have changed in the last few years, but I'm confident that the relative comparison with the other parts of the UK remains true, and we can still agree with the BBC when it calls us a comparative *"bastion of marriage.*[24] Bear in mind that Northern Ireland does this without the relatively large Islamic population present in the rest of the UK, who have much higher marriage rates than ethnic Brits and thereby inflate the figures to a certain degree.[25]

---

[22] https://macdor.co.uk/northern-ireland-marriage-rates-locations/
https://www.ons.gov.uk/peoplepopulationandcommunity/birthsdeathsandmarriages/marriagecohabitationandcivilpartnerships/bulletins/marriagesinenglandandwalesprovisional/2017
https://www.cso.ie/en/releasesandpublications/er/mar/marriages2019/
all accessed 14th December 2021
[23] https://www.bbc.co.uk/relationships/tv_and_radio/love_map/ukmaplove_nireland.shtml accessed 14th December 2021
[24] ibid
[25]
https://singlemuslim.com/pages/news/PR/News/ukmarriagetrendsshowmuslimsmorecommittedtomarriage accessed 14th December w021

My brother, who lives in some God-forsaken city called something like 'London' got married recently. He's twenty-six, and most of his friends are around the same age. As someone who has lived in England for a decade, most of them are also unfortunately English. I had the privilege to be his best-man, and therefore got to hang out with many of them during his stag and his wedding, which was honestly great craic, and they were a nice bunch. However during the course of events, we got into conversation, and not only were none of the English contingent married or engaged, none of the ones I spoke with had even *been to a wedding*. At least, not in their memory. That is to say, this group of mid-to-late-twenty-somethings had no close friends or family members who had gotten married during their teenage or adult years. That's utterly bonkers.

Northern Irish family values don't stop at marriage. Unlike much of the Western world, we actually still like kids. That's not some sarcastic remark; most of the Western world is actively anti-child, viewing them as a problem to be solved and a burden to be carried, rather than a blessing to enjoy.

Whilst Northern Irish birth rates are on the decrease, we still have around twelve births per thousand inhabitants, which is a little bit higher than the rest of the UK, which sits at eleven births per thousand.[26] Similar to marriage rates, UK birth numbers are again bolstered by a comparatively large Islamic population, who give birth at about twice the rate of ethnic Brits, and without which my maths tells me that the UK birth rate would be more like ten per thousand.[27] (By the way, I say all

---

[26] https://www.macrotrends.net/countries/GBR/united-kingdom/birth-rate
[27] https://www.thetimes.co.uk/article/rise-in-muslim-birthrate-as-families-feel-british-l2l0v8cm7pf
https://www.theguardian.com/news/datablog/2014/jan/10/rise-british-muslim-birthrate-the-times-census
both accessed 14th December 2021

this as a positive about the Islamic community, not in an 'Oh Billy, they're coming for us' kind of way.) Canada also has ten births per thousand, as does the Netherlands and Austria, Germany has nine, Portugal, Finland and Spain have eight, and Italy has just seven.[28]

But it's not just the birth-rates of each nation that show our comparative love for kids; it's also the overall setup of our society. The sheer inaffordability of the mainland UK means that two parents must work full time to simply own a home of any sort, whilst their kids are raised by day-care workers and schoolteachers. Not so in Northern Ireland, where we have some of the most affordable cities in the UK, and unlike other cheap UK cities, ours are actually nice to live in.[29] We have kid-friendly activities everywhere: great parks, soft-play areas, green spaces and sports clubs. Schools are often smaller, with vastly more parent-teacher interaction than the faceless child-factories on the mainland. In my experience, businesses also cater to kids and parents at a far greater rate than the rest of the UK, with child-discounts, kids' specials and a general sense that buggies, toddlers and silly laughs are welcomed rather than despised. As I said, we actually like kids here.

A Christian culture under threat

The religiosity of Northern Ireland, the focus on the local and our family values, are all the result of having a culture significantly impacted by Christianity. Some might push back on that, rightly asking, "But what about the historic violence and division?" Sure, that has

---

[28] https://data.worldbank.org/indicator/SP.DYN.CBRT.IN?most_recent_value_desc=false accessed 14th December 2021
[29] https://news.sky.com/story/revealed-the-uks-least-and-most-affordable-cities-12378781 accessed 14th December 2021

been the result of a culture impacted by an erroneous faith, where Christ was acknowledged with lips but absent in hearts. False Christianity, unchristlike Christianity - a contradiction in terms - impacts culture too. But if we can acknowledge that there are cultural downsides to the false Christianity present in our history, we can also acknowledge the cultural benefits of the true Christianity which sat alongside it. We still see the impact of both in Northern Ireland today.

Now as Northern Ireland seeks to rebuild a cultural identity no longer marked by sectarian violence and division, the thing to do would be to attempt to maintain the benefits of our historic Christian culture and dispense with the drawbacks our past has left us. Let's have a Christian society, but filled with true Christianity, lived out in every sphere. Let's have a society where we care about our neighbours, all of them, regardless of their cultural background. Let's have a society where we care about families, including the families of the 'other side'. Our history might contain a fair bit of manky bathwater, but there's a happy, wriggling baby in there somewhere.

Unfortunately we've sought to enlarge the drain sufficiently to swallow said baby whole.

In Ulster society today, particularly as one looks higher up the economic ladder and further down the age spectrum, there is a sense of shame over anything seen as robustly Northern Irish. Incorrectly tying all our historical and cultural norms to the Troubles, a large portion of Northern Irish upper-middle classes and our Millennial-and-younger age-groups assume that anything resembling a defence or a celebration of Northern Irish culture is a call to division and hatred. It's a common view that working-class Ulstermen-and-women who are proud of their heritage - particularly on the Protestant side - are a bunch of bigots. (Which seems like an acute form of bigotry, but I digress.) In an attempt to curry an air of respectability among the outside world, many feel they must reject all things Northern Irish, including the positives like our religious devotion, our love for the local, and our family values. Though many of this group are sincere Christians, they are as exuberant as any ardent atheist in throwing off the alleged shackles of the Christian worldview that underpins the advantages of Northern Irish culture. Ashamed of the history of their Somewhere, they try to make themselves Anywheres.

There are scenarios where a society abandoning much its culture and extensively embracing a new one from the outside world is a positive thing. For instance, it doesn't matter how important of a cultural ritual cannibalism is, or how delicious you think tasty-but-lost explorers are, it would be objectively better to abandon that cultural norm and embrace a bit of Anywhere-ism. So if the outside world was a more Christian place, if we lived in a world where religion was more sincere and Christlike, if we lived in a world where connecting to your local community was more important than it was to us, if we lived in a world that valued family more than we do, then we would be better off embracing the Anywhere over our Somewhere. A Somewhere is not necessarily better just by virtue of being a Somewhere.

But we are living in a time of massive cultural upheaval in the Western world, and the Anywhere is becoming an increasingly dark and ominous place, particularly for anyone who either wants to be a faithful

Christian, or who believes that Christianity is a cultural force for good.

Aaron Renn, a Christian sociologist, divides the recent history of the Western world into three phases: the Christian-positive world, the Christian-neutral world, and the Christian-negative world.[30] Though he applies this to an American context, the same pattern has played out in a similar way in Northern Ireland, and furthermore the US has been the dominant cultural power in the West for some time now, meaning that our immediate external cultural milieu is strongly impacted by events across the Atlantic. So if we want to see how we got here and where we're headed, it's worth looking at.

Renn argues that the Christian-positive culture exists where being seen as religious and following traditional Christian morality is a social positive, where Christianity is a status enhancer, and in some cases failure to embrace those norms is detrimental.[31] You could argue that the Christian-positive world existed in Ireland from the time of St Patrick, when the gospel swept the nation in a profound move of God that shaped Irish history from the early fifth century. Indeed, it's hard to argue anything else. The argument was not over whether Christianity should be accepted as the moral and social standard, but which form of Christianity. Looking at it from a modern American perspective, Renn cites figures like Pat Robertson, Oral Roberts, the Bakkers, and Jerry Falwell as important, typical Christian-positive world figures.[32] He also believes that

---

[30] https://www.aaronrenn.com/wp-content/uploads/2018/03/The-Masculinist-13-The-Lost-World-of-American-Evangelicalism.pdf accessed 14th December 2021
[31] ibid
[32] ibid

the tipping point that marked the end of this period in America was around 1994, when the first accusations of sexual misconduct were made against President Bill Clinton, and yet he maintained his role in office.[33] In a Northern Irish context, similar Christian-positive-world figures would likely include Dr Ian Paisley and James McConnell on the Protestant side, and on the Catholic side (which is more position-driven than personality-driven) would include popes, bishops and priests. Similar to America, this period probably ended in Northern Ireland for Catholics in the mid-1990s, as rumours of abuse within the Catholic church began to stir, and perhaps for Protestants the Good Friday Agreement on 10th April 1998 might be an appropriate marker, when people seemed to tire of anything perceived to be religious dogmatism.[34]

A Christian-neutral world, according to Renn, is one where being seen as religious is a morally neutral attribute, a kind of personal hobby or interest, and time in which traditional norms have a degree of historic momentum but are not necessarily propagated. I would say that this world aligns neatly with the cultural rise of 'soft-postmodernism' - an ideology that basically requires that you should be a decent person, believe what you like, be sincere, and don't push it too hard on anyone else. Renn postulates that key figures of the Western Christian-neutral world included Hillsong and Timothy Keller, and though he places the seeker-sensitive movement in the positive world - where it definitely had its origins - we can objectively say that it had its heyday in the neutral world. Realistically, the

---

[33] ibid
[34] Gribben, Crawford, *The Rise And Fall Of Christian Ireland*, page 163-198

emergent church also had a twenty-minute blaze of incoherent glory at some point towards the latter end of this period. For Northern Ireland, the Christian neutral world was centred around the Charismatic movement, which again, started in the positive world, but was probably most influential in the late-90s through the 00s until somewhere in the 2010s. Churches like Christian Fellowship Church Belfast and Causeway Coast Vineyard led the way in this, with many denominational leaders also embracing this movement in places like Fisherwick Presbyterian Church, Carnmoney Presbyterian Church, and Willowfield Parish Church. Interestingly, this movement on the Protestant side was often connected to more ecumenical Christianity and a corresponding Charismatic renewal in the Catholic church; exemplified in organisations like Shalom House and Corrymeela.[35]

As the 'soft-postmodernism' gradually but inevitably hardened into what pastor-theologian Douglas Wilson calls '*totalitolerance*', the Christian-neutral world came to an end, giving way to a Christian-negative world.[36] In this world, being seen as a Christian, particularly one who holds to traditional Christian morality, is seen as a social negative, such moral norms are expressly rejected, and Christianity is seen as a threat to the social good.[37] Renn places the emergence of the Christian-negative world in around 2014, when support for same-sex marriage was gaining unstoppable momentum, before being ratified into law in the 'Obergefell' Supreme Court

---

[35] http://shalomhouse.org.uk/about-us accessed 15th December 2021
https://www.corrymeela.org/ accessed 15th December 2021
[36] https://dougwils.com/books-and-culture/s7-engaging-the-culture/totalitolerance.html accessed 15th December 2021
[37] https://www.aaronrenn.com/wp-content/uploads/2018/03/The-Masculinist-13-The-Lost-World-of-American-Evangelicalism.pdf accessed 14th December 2021

decision the following year.[38] For Catholics in the Republic of Ireland, and to some extent also in Northern Ireland, this world formed in around 2009, when the scandals involving sexual abuse, illegal adoption and financial misconduct were revealed in the Murphy Report.[39] Support for Catholic values has since vanished at an astounding rate across the island, particularly south of the border.[40] In the Protestant community, one could argue that the same issue which led to an American Christian-negative world has also led to a Northern Irish one, with the Ashers Baking Company 'gay cake' case of the late 2010s, and the Westminster act legalising same-sex marriage and abortion across the province in 2019.[41] Known Christian figures that reflect the church in this world don't yet exist, because we have only just entered into it, seemingly with our trousers wrapped firmly round our ankles.

To add my own little tidbit to Renn's cultural analysis (aside from the Northern Irish application, which I had to think through myself because for some inexplicable reason he never addressed us directly) I think we can recognise much of the difference between these worlds in the way evangelism has been done. Evangelism in Christian-positive world was the work of preachers; Billy Graham in particular, and everyone else who basically wanted to be Billy Graham. The church evangelised by holding a special meeting of some sort and inviting people to hear a hot-gospel preacher. Nothing wrong with that at all. In the neutral world, evangelism was much more oriented around

---

[38] https://www.supremecourt.gov/opinions/14pdf/14-556_3204.pdf accessed 15th December 2021
[39] https://www.justice.ie/en/JELR/Pages/PB09000504 accessed 15th December 2021
[40] https://www.bbc.co.uk/news/uk-northern-ireland-politics-56041849 accessed 15th December 2021
[41] https://www.christian.org.uk/case/ashers-baking-company/ accessed 15th December 2021

respectability and relationships; we do church well, we are smart and nice people, so hear us out. Bible teachers rather than Bible-preachers were in vogue; the same truth (usually) but in a less confrontational style. Again, nothing wrong with that either. If you're looking for examples, think 'Alpha'. Coming to today's society, I don't believe that there's a coherent strategy in place for the church in a Christian-negative world just yet, but allow me to jump ahead of myself in the broader flow of this book and make a suggestion. Whilst we're not remotely done with gospel preaching, relationships or excellence, we're going to need to add a fair whack of legitimate courage and counter-cultural resistance.

All that to say, Northern Irish culture is under threat from a Christian-negative Anywhere world that has exactly zero respect for religion, local attachments, or family values. Case in point: the aforementioned same-sex marriage and abortion act of 2019, which flies in the face of both Protestant and Catholic religious morality, is a direct attack on the family values of our province, and was imposed on us not by our local government, but by a English Labour politician in London.[42] The wider Western world is being carried off on a tidal wave of secularism that will not stop until everything is washed away, Northern Ireland included, and it is already breaching our floodgates.

Unfortunately the threat to our common culture already exists to some extent within on our own shores. Looking across our political parties, for instance, the correct response is something like utter despair.

Sinn Féin is on course to be the largest party in Northern Ireland and is overwhelmingly voted for by

---

[42] https://www.bbc.co.uk/news/uk-northern-ireland-politics-56041849 accessed 15th December 2021

the province's Catholic community, but has never in its entire history been the slightest bit Catholic. Birthed in the Easter Rising of 1916, the Catholic church stood against this violent form of Republicanism, claiming it did not meet the criteria for Christian 'just war'.[43] From its inception, Sinn Féin has openly supported the Irish Republican Army, an organisation universally and repeatedly condemned by Catholic bishops and priests as far back as 1926, then again officially in 1931, and further echoed by Pope John Paul II on his visit to Dublin in 1979.[44] The IRA rejected ecclesiastical calls to end violence for half a century, and Sinn Féin chose the paramilitaries over the church. In addition to this, the party has been economically socialist from its inception, something once again formally repudiated by the Irish Catholic church as contrary to its central tenets.[45] Sinn Féin has more recently demonstrated fervent political support for abortion and same-sex marriage in Ireland on both sides of the border, both of which are explicitly condemned by official Catholic teaching.[46] Though from time to time the party has used Catholic rhetoric as a means to its political ends, it has been clear from their actions that their true allegiance lies with revolutionary Marxism and cultural leftism, not the Vatican.[47]

The Alliance Party was at one point an acceptable Christian political option, rejecting Northern Irish sectarian politics, pursuing peace and showing respect for both sides. However it has since embraced almost every position of global cultural leftism, marching

---

[43] Crawford Gribben, *The Rise And Fall Of Christian Ireland*, 168
[44] Ibid, 174, 180, 196
[45] Ibid, 180
[46] Ibid, 208, https://www.bbc.co.uk/news/av/uk-northern-ireland-48937481 accessed 15th December 2021
[47] Crawford Gribben, *The Rise And Fall Of Christian Ireland*, 186

lockstep with Sinn Féin and the totalitarian progressives on issues of abortion, religious freedom and marriage. The Alliance Party took a clear stance against Ashers Bakery in the entirely frivolous lawsuit against them for refusing to print a pro-gay-marriage slogan on a cake, and was not only a leading advocate for legalising abortion in Northern Ireland, but was at the forefront of the initiative to outlaw prayer and Christian witness within an undefined buffer zone near abortion clinics.[48] At one point the Alliance Party was neither anti-Catholic nor anti-Protestant, but now it is in danger of becoming functionally anti-Christian. Furthermore much of the Alliance Party epitomises the desire to be seen as sophisticated by overseas elites, thus viewing anything quintessentially Ulster as a hangover of bigotry, and the perception among the working classes is that the Alliance Party is at best detached from their communities, or at worst has open disdain for them. Their plans for the province look much less like a unique culture embodying the best of Northern Irish history, and much more like a cookie-cutter part of a secular global community with no distinct identity of our own.

Some might think that the DUP could rescue Northern Irish culture, and they are certainly better than either of the above on issues of the family and religious freedom. However, there is still a broad tendency across the party to cling to the old prejudices, bringing everything from the negative past of Northern Irish culture with them into 21st century politics.[49] Their vehement opposition to the Irish language when juxtaposed with their

---

[48] https://www.belfasttelegraph.co.uk/news/northern-ireland/sinn-fein-send-solidarity-to-lgbt-community-after-disappointing-ashers-ruling-37405521.html accessed 15th December 2021
https://www.belfasttelegraph.co.uk/news/health/safe-zones-plan-to-halt-abortion-intimidation-40368006.html accessed 15th December 2021
[49] https://www.bbc.co.uk/news/uk-northern-ireland-29895593 accessed 15th December 2021

comparatively tepid response to the slaughter of the unborn shows a serious lack of Christian priorities. The first brought the DUP almost to the point of shutting down the Northern Irish assembly, the latter to bluster and little else.[50] Though I prefer blustery opposition to killing unborn children to the outright advocacy of the other parties, flipping tables would have been a better response, and a government shutdown in this instance would have been much more defensible than over the Irish language. Furthermore, though they purport to stand in defence of Northern Irish culture, they consistently only do so for half of the population, and even for the half that they allegedly represent, their desire to place the Union above the province in the Brexit protocol has exposed how they have become drawn to global power over local responsibility.[51] All that doesn't even mention the ungodly stink of a large portion of the party's leadership, many of them professing Christians, stealing tens of millions in taxpayer money in the Renewable Heating Incentive scandal.[52]

In short, they're all pretty wick, and they all need to repent. But everyone already knows that.

(Let me momentarily acknowledge that there are likely sincere believers involved with each of these parties. Similarly, there were individual Pharisees who sincerely followed Jesus. Just as these righteous individuals would have agreed with Jesus' assessment of the Pharisees as a group, believers involved in any of

---

[50] https://www.theguardian.com/politics/2021/jun/14/irish-language-row-threatens-to-derail-northern-ireland-government accessed 15th December 2021
https://www.bbc.co.uk/news/uk-northern-ireland-politics-56041850 accessed 15th December 2021
[51] https://www.newsletter.co.uk/news/opinion/letters/the-dup-support-for-a-regulatory-border-in-the-irish-sea-in-2019-was-a-catastrophic-error-one-of-the-worst-unionist-mis-judgements-of-recent-history-3398432 accessed 15th December 2021
[52] https://www.bbc.co.uk/news/uk-northern-ireland-38301428 accessed 15th December 2021

those parties should agree with a biblical analysis of them and throw everything into party reform. If reform is not possible, leaving always is.)

All that is good about Northern Ireland is not merely being attacked from the outside, but those at the most important levels of government, culture and media, have done little to defend it from the inside. At the risk of saying something patently obvious, the pathway to Northern Ireland becoming all that we could and should be, something in line with the good of our past but rejecting the bad, doesn't lie with any our political parties.

That said, I definitely don't wish to 'black-pill' everyone into a state of hopelessness. Much good remains in our province. I mentioned earlier about our large number of devout Christians; if we could get our act together somewhat and start evangelising, discipling and building culture, we would be a blessing to the nation as a whole. Furthermore, unlike the stringently secular societies I have also lived in - Southern England and Sweden - Northern Ireland has not completely downed the progressive Slush Puppy and requested another, brain-freeze be blasted. There's a fair amount of common sense here, something apparently uncommon elsewhere, and a reasonable chance that when a Northern Irish person is told an obvious porky by some new cultural elite - perhaps about how many new genders there are or how tolerance really means suing anyone who disagrees with you into oblivion - that the response will be something like, "Aye, bog off." Perhaps with a stronger word than 'bog'. Given the alternatives, I'll take the Northern Irish course language with common sense over some well-spoken moral insanity.

The Northern Irish common culture is under threat, and may be wounded, but it is certainly not dead. There is a lot that can be rescued and perhaps a fresh expression of our religious heritage, our local emphasis and our family values to be revealed. Our province is both saveable and worth saving. The solution doesn't lie with our politicians, it lies with our King. And He'll use His body to do it. The question is: is the church up to the challenge?

Oh flip.

Discussion Questions

1 – What is your favourite aspect of Northern Irish culture, and why? How do you see something of God at work in our nation in that area?

2 – What is your least favourite aspect of Northern Irish culture, and why? How do you see something of sin or the devil at work in that area in our nation?

3 – Have you ever considered that a culture can or should be Christian, and what does that mean?

4 – Have you noticed the change in attitudes towards the church in our culture, and if so, how?

CHAPTER 3
BOYS A DEAR

Or: The Current State Of The Northern Irish Church

You've probably seen a family destroyed by the dad. I know I've seen several, and heard of countless more. In one case, it was drink. Not necessarily getting blind drunk or flying into uncontrolled, booze-fuelled fits; I didn't hear about that. But the consistent presence of alcohol, the inability to even walk the dog without a can of something or other, the regular driving under the influence, the money spent, the obvious depressive anxiety when he didn't have a least a bit of a buzz, the half-cut oversharing, the words spoken too quickly that couldn't be retracted, the mockery, the supposedly funny but actually just aggressive sarcasm, the jovial encouragement towards his own kids to take up the habit, the fact that they did because no teenager turns down the offer of free liquor and no discipline - all of this conspired to take what should have been a healthy, purportedly Christian marriage, with what should have been believing children, and tore the whole thing apart. The wife ended up alone, the debt mounted, the kids were either scared of him or didn't respect him, and seeing as their dad still claimed the Name of Christ, that Name was mud to them. The thing is, the wife was a wonderful believer. She prayed, attended church, served, gave, loved, studied Scripture, and tried to make the best of it. If any woman could have turned the direction of her family for good in such a scenario, it would have been her. But, for good or ill, man is the head of the home.

We often think that the Bible says the man *should be* the head of the home. Ok, some of you more progressive types might think that Bible says nothing of the sort, but you've got to do some crazy hermeneutical gymnastics to get there, and this isn't a book on that topic, so I won't get sidetracked. But for those of us who read the words that *'the husband is head of the wife'* (Eph 5:23, 1 Cor. 11:3) and think that it means something like *'the husband is head of the wife'* - i.e. the obvious understanding - even though we accept it, often view it as an ideal. We think it means the husband should be the head of the wife, he should strive to set the spiritual tone of the home, that a godly man's aim is to be the household leader. But that's not what the text says. The text doesn't say that the husband *should be* the head of the home, it says that the husband *is* the head of the home. He will either do it intentionally or unintentionally, he will either do it well or badly, he will either do it like Jesus or like a devil, but nothing at all, not even his own abdication, can stop him from doing it. He sets the direction. Even if he is absent, his empty chair is the centre of gravity in that household.

To give a counter example, I am acquainted with a pastor whose wife, I later heard, backslid entirely, rejected the faith, had multiple ongoing affairs, would not stop, refused to be reconciled to him despite his best efforts, and so they divorced. Obviously I don't know the whole story, but that much is common knowledge. But the kids have not fallen apart the way most would. By some miracle the dad got custody, which is extraordinarily rare, and from everything I can tell his kids are devoted to him, love him, are thriving, and fully involved in his great church. He has remarried a godly woman who is part of their church, and they seem every bit a happy family. Even if a woman attempts to take a sledgehammer to her entire family unit, it's no match for the resoluteness of a godly man.

Now, that is not to say mothers have no influence or that great mothers cannot do great good. If a mother in an unbelieving family comes to faith, there's a 17% chance that the rest of the family will eventually make a commitment.[53] That's almost one in five, that's awesome, that's influence, and if that's you, be encouraged: you can make a difference. But if a father in an unbelieving family comes to faith, there's a 93% chance the rest will make a commitment.[54] That's not just influence, that's headship. There's a reasonable chance that the 17% reflects families where the dad shows a degree of openness, and the reality is that a mother will almost never overcome the power of a father wholeheartedly travelling in the opposite direction. If she succeeds, it is a miracle every bit as great as someone successfully kayaking the Niagara Falls. Upwards. We serve a God who works such miracles, so we would never say never, but we have to recognise how great such miracles are. In bad situations, often the only way for a woman to succeed in breaking the influence of a destructive dad is to invoke the power of the state in her favour, and even then, a determined father often finds a way. It literally takes a mum plus an army to even have a chance at overcoming a dad. The Bible does not call

---

[53] https://www.baptistpress.com/resource-library/news/want-your-church-to-grow-then-bring-in-the-men/ accessed 15th December 2021
[54] Ibid, accessed 15th December 2021

men to lead their families; it says that men do lead their families and calls them to do it well.

Now with that concept in mind, and remembering that this is supposed to be a book about revival in Northern Ireland and not about a Christian view of marriage, read the following words from Jesus:

> *You are the salt of the earth, but if salt has lost its taste, how shall its saltiness be restored? It is no longer good for anything except to be thrown out and trampled under people's feet. "You are the light of the world. A city set on a hill cannot be hidden. Nor do people light a lamp and put it under a basket, but on a stand, and it gives light to all in the house. In the same way, let your light shine before others, so that they may see your good works and give glory to your Father who is in heaven.*
>
> (Matthew 5:13-16)

Did you catch it? Let me repeat the key phrases with altered emphasis and see if you get it. "You *are* the salt of the earth.... You *are* the light of the world..."

I've heard a lot made in various sermons as to what being the salt of the earth means; is preservative, flavour, maybe even a primitive form of fertiliser? But I think we've often missed the enormity of this claim. It's not just telling us something *to do*, it is telling us something *we are*; we are the salt of the earth, we are the light of the world. The Bible does not say that we should try and determine the saltiness or the brightness of the world; it tells us that we do. We are not called to be salt and light; we are salt and light, and we are called to maintain our flavour and shine brightly.

In this passage, Jesus is telling His people that they actually determine the direction of the society around them. We often think that the church has little power over the surrounding culture; Jesus says that we are the engine that drives the surrounding culture. Like a man in his home, we will either do so intentionally or unintentionally, well or badly, in line with Scripture or against it - but we cannot fail to do it. If the church maintains its saltiness, the world around us will be salted, whether it likes it or not; if the church shines brightly, the world around us will be lit, whether it likes it or not.

At the root of every culture is the 'cultus' - the Latin term for worship. Religion is not some subsection of the culture, like your granny's good china that sits off in glass cabinet somewhere, the latter of which she uses to confuse everyone by referring to it using terms like 'armoire' or 'chifforobe', with the fancy plates to be brought out at certain times of the year when everyone tries to behave like civilised adults. We often think that the majority of the nation views religion like that, and to be fair the 'official religion' of a nation often is viewed like that; an ornate decoration which is there for appearances and special occasions, but which is minimally used. However the real religion of the nation, the thing that it actually holds in highest value, is the wellspring and focal point of the entire culture. A culture that worships Allah will be driven by that; a culture that worships money will be driven by that; a culture that worships tolerance will be driven by that: and a culture that worships self will be driven by that. The church is explicitly called to an aggressive invasion of this epicentre of culture in every nation across the globe and to make Christ the object of worship there, a process the Bible describes as 'making disciples of all nations'. As the church captures the locus of culture by fulfilling this Great Commission, it simply cannot do anything other than radically transform the society around it.

Now with all of this talk about the church setting the spiritual tone for the nation in spite of the world's resistance, some of you may wonder, "What about nations where they have another object of worship? Surely we can't say that the church is failing to be salt there by definition. Or what about faithful churches in godless cultures, where they are persecuted, despised and rejected? Are you accusing them of lacking saltiness?" Not at all. You've just assumed I'm talking about a shorter-term perspective than I actually am. We often measure the progress of the church in years; we'd be better thinking about it in millennia. It took three hundred years for the church to meaningfully impact Roman society, many more centuries for the rest of Europe, and even then its aberrant teaching and moral compromise made its influence less pervasive than it should have been. Though it can be a slow process, if we can maintain our flavour and our brightness across the ages, the world will ultimately be transformed for good as the gospel wins the nations. Alternatively, if we become sinful, compromised and cowardly, if we are flavourless salt and hidden light, then we are just like the dark and savourless world around us, having no effect. But if so, the issue is not that the world is unwilling to obey Christ; the issue is that the *church* is unwilling to do so. For good or ill, the church bears primary responsibility for the overall direction of the culture over time. Jesus says that a salty church *will* make the world salty, and a shining church *will* make the world bright - full stop.

At every point along the way we must ensure that we have played our part in this: maintaining our flavour and shining brightly. We would be particularly wise to check if we have done so if we were to see a culture in which, after a long period of widespread Christian worship and a universally accepted Christian worldview, that worship and worldview were being left behind at a rate of knots. If a nation seems to be in a process of completely de-salting itself - or desalinisation, a word the internet tells me exists - then we might just have a low-sodium church on our hands. So, Christians of Northern Ireland, how are we doing?

Erm, whoops - the recent past

Well our recent history is not exactly great. As I've already said, I'm not a Catholic, and have major disagreements with Catholic beliefs, but at the same time no analysis of the Northern Irish church would be complete without mentioning the stunning collapse of Roman Catholicism on this island. So we'll start there.

Irish Catholicism grew from a relatively nominal faith in the early 1800s to the dominant cultural force of Ireland a century later. There were multiple reasons for this, but one key factor was a project known as '*Catholic Action*' which sought to establish Catholic social teaching in every sphere of society.[55] It succeeded.[56] They wrote serious books about the framework of a Christian nation, trained clergy, led the way in Gaelic

---

[55] Crawford Gribben, *The Rise And Fall Of Christian Ireland,*, 174-176
[56] Ibid, 174-176

society, organised papal visits attended by up to one-third of the island's population, and much more - all in an effort to establish Ireland as a distinctly Catholic nation.[57] The results were astounding: in 1834 only 40% of Irish Catholics regularly attended mass, but throughout the 1900s it was up around 90%, and often higher.[58]

(I'm aware this book is about Northern Ireland, but part of the reason for Northern Irish Catholics' affinity with the Republic comes back to this determined effort to create a faith-based society in this time. It's impossible to speak about Northern Irish Catholics without referring to them as part of the overall Irish Catholic church.)

But this attendance has since fallen off a cliff. Though 78% of the nation still identify as Catholic, they have thrown off Catholic teaching and practice, and in 2011, just 30% of Irish Catholics regularly attended mass.[59] Irish seminaries, which long produced an exceptionally high number of Catholic priesthood for the size of the overall population, *"could not close fast enough to cope with decreasing demand,"* according to historian Crawford Gribben.[60] Catholic social teaching has been explicitly rejected; a nation where same-sex activity was illegal until 1995 became the first in the world to legalise same-

---

[57] Ibid, 174-180
[58] Ibid, 156
https://www.historyireland.com/20th-century-contemporary-history/a-church-in-crisis/
https://theweek.com/articles/445823/everything-need-know-about-irelands-disaffected-catholics
https://www.irishtimes.com/news/social-affairs/religion-and-beliefs/the-faith-of-ireland-s-catholics-continues-despite-all-1.3592019
all accessed 16th December 2021
[59] Crawford Gribben, *The Rise And Fall Of Christian Ireland*, 205, 206
https://www.irishtimes.com/news/social-affairs/religion-and-beliefs/the-faith-of-ireland-s-catholics-continues-despite-all-1.3592019
accessed 15th December 2021
[60] Crawford Gribben, *The Rise And Fall Of Christian Ireland*, 206 - excuse a slight rewording to adjust for context

sex marriage by popular vote in 2015, and the nationwide ban on abortion was overturned by a two-thirds majority in 2018.[61] It turned out that the appearance of faith held by the large majority of Irish Catholics was paper thin.

You could argue that recent Western Protestantism has lacked an emphasis on cultural transformation, and made the whole thing solely about personal faith, shrinking the kingdom of God down to something that only exists in the heart and not in the wider world. However Irish Catholicism's demise has demonstrated that a cultural faith, however historically rich, theologically grounded and thoroughly implemented, but which is not centred around personal trust in Jesus, is a hollow shell. To the naked eye the whole thing may look fine, but apply the slightest hint of pressure and it crushes to bits in your hand. The foundation of a Christian nation is individual salvation. Protestants on this island have perhaps dug out a rock-solid foundation but neglected to build much upon it. The Catholics, on the other hand, were busy building an enormous edifice, but decided the best place for it was a wet bog somewhere in Donegal. The storm came and the house build on sand, or rather peat, crashed in a heap.

What, however, was the catalyst for this collapse? It didn't come out of nowhere. I'll give you a hint: it wasn't something outside the church.

No, rather the moral authority of the church was, as Gribben puts it, "*shattered by a devastating sequence of scandals.*"[62] Beginning the mid-90s, where multiple notable Catholic clergy where exposed as having secret

---

[61] Ibid 206, https://www.bbc.com/news/world-europe-44256152 accessed 16th December 2021
[62] Crawford Gribben, *The Rise And Fall Of Christian Ireland,*, 200

families, and during which time increasing numbers of stories of abuse of children and single mothers by the clergy, trust in the church as an institution began to erode. But these revelations merely scratched the surface. Though only six priests had been convicted of abuse between the years of 1975 and 2011, it became clear that during that time period 'hundreds of priests had been abusing thousands of people in their care.'[63] The Ferns Report (2005) and the Ryan and Murphy Reports (both 2009) dug deep and found the extent of the evil, describing how orphanages, hostels and schools became sites of 'systemic exploitation, trafficking, malnutrition, sexual abuse and death'.[64] The worst of these was described by then-Taoiseach Enda Kenny as a *'chamber of horrors'* - with skeletons of babies killed by malnutrition found on the site of an institution from which one-thousand further children were illegally trafficked to America without the consent or knowledge of their mothers in a kids-for-cash adoption scheme.[65] The voice of moral clarity in the nation came not from the priests but from the politicians, and a moving speech from the aforementioned Kenny, in one moment, shifted the moral centre of the nation from the church to the state, functionally ending Catholic Ireland almost overnight.[66] If the salt loses its flavour...

The fall of Protestantism has been much slower than that of Catholicism, but started from a lower height. In Northern Ireland, weekly church attendance fell from over 60% of the population in 1968 to just over 40% in 2004.[67] That includes both Catholic and Protestant

---

[63] Ibid, 202
[64] Crawford Gribben, *The Rise And Fall Of Christian Ireland,*, 203
[65] Ibid, 203-204
[66] Ibid, 205
[67] Ibid, 200

attendance, but seeing as the North had a large Protestant majority throughout that time, and Catholic church attendance didn't start to plummet until after that time, this was likely reflective of Protestant church decrease. We know for sure that 52% of Protestants attended church weekly in 1998, compared to 43% in 2017 - which would map onto the former trajectory of presumed Protestant church decline neatly.[68] To its detriment, Protestantism in the North was never as successful as Catholicism in the South at generating almost ubiquitous church attendance among its professing adherents. But in its favour, Protestantism hasn't fallen off a cliff in the way that Catholicism has, at least not yet, likely due to higher levels of genuine personal faith among Protestants, and not having a scandal at the same scale as Irish Catholicism. That said, it's hard to believe that there isn't a cliff edge up ahead. We shouldn't get smug just because we're driving towards it at fifty miles per hour whilst the Catholics drove there at eighty.

Through a couple of different treaties and bills, the island of Ireland was partitioned into Southern Ireland (later the Republic of Ireland), an overwhelmingly Catholic 'Free State', and Northern Ireland, which was governed by what many, including its proponents, termed as a 'protestant parliament for a protestant people'.[69] As a firm believer in Protestant soteriology, I would be delighted to say that the Protestant majority in the North sought to reach and convince the remaining Catholic third of the province with gospel preaching,

---

[68] https://sluggerotoole.com/2018/07/01/doctrine-and-decline-irish-churches-and-the-conservative-turn/ accessed 16th December 2021
[69] Crawford Gribben, *The Rise And Fall Of Christian Ireland,*, 169

good works, just systems and sincere neighbourly love. Unfortunately, they did pretty much the opposite.

There's been a lot of discussion as to the extent of Protestant discrimination against Catholics in Northern Ireland.[70] How much of it was an intentional system to create a subclass, how much was ingrained bias but not necessarily an organised effort, and how much of the gap was due to other factors? And in an era when there was legitimate concern about Republican claims on Northern Ireland being backed up by military force, with a section of the population likely supporting a potential Irish invasion, how should the Northern Irish political system have functioned?[71]

Nonetheless, it's still a question of how much discrimination, not whether there was any, and the consensus is that it was extensive. Prejudice was rife in the job market, with Protestants particularly keen to prevent Catholics from holding public sector jobs. For instance in 1968 in Fermanagh, no senior council posts were held by Catholics, and of the 370 posts available, 322 were held by Protestants - an amazing number seeing as Fermanagh was majority Catholic at the time.[72] Or consider how in 1982 at Harland and Wolff, one of the province's top employers, there was not a single Catholic engineer, and I'm pretty sure there were at least *some* Catholics interested in the field...[73] Housing was another area of notable partisanship, with Catholics being forbidden from living in certain areas, overlooked for council housing, and forced to live in regions where

---

[70] https://cain.ulster.ac.uk/issues/discrimination/gudgin99.htm
https://cain.ulster.ac.uk/issues/discrimination/whyte.htm
Both accessed 16th December 2021
[71] https://www.irishtimes.com/opinion/operation-armageddon-would-have-been-doomsday-for-irish-aggressors-1.728983 accessed 16th December 2021
[72] Mike Commins, Northern Ireland-Britain's Legacy, (Resourcefulmedia.uk, 2019) page 69
[73] Ibid, page 69

the Unionist vote was strongest to ensure parliamentary majorities.[74] And if you've ever heard the term 'gerrymandering' and wondered what it meant, well, it's not a dude called Jerry, surname Mandering, but the process of tweaking election boundaries to get the right outcome. There was a whole lot of this going on to nullify the Catholic vote.[75]

Then there's Ian Paisley. What on earth do you do with a man like that? Before I attempt to do anything at all with him, allow me to address the fact that I can't win here. There are two groups among my (likely) evangelical readership, kudos to you if you aren't in that group by the way, great to have you with us. Firstly there are those who think Paisley was a Protestant saint, a bulwark against evil, someone who stood up to terrorism, and led a revival. Then there are those who are either so embarrassed by him that they can't squeeze out a single word in his favour, or they expel him from the kingdom entirely.

The answer probably lies somewhere in the middle. Obviously we can't speak to the state of anyone's soul, but we can look at the external evidence. In that regard, Paisley was clearly a fervent Bible-believer who preached the word, reached the lost, prayed like a whirlwind and led a movement that still has positive effects on Northern Irish Christianity today. If you disagree, I challenge you to listen to some of his sermons on YouTube and tell me that isn't a man on fire for God. Furthermore, he was renowned for being a wonderful and impartial constituency MP, helping Catholics with minor issues as readily as Protestants, and welcoming

---

[74] Ibid, page 76
[75] page 77

The Coming Ulster Revival

Catholics into his home to pray for them.[76] Yet he's also the man who said things about Catholics like, *"They breed like rabbits and multiply like vermin,"* and, in response to attacks on Catholic homes, claimed, *"Catholic homes caught fire because they were loaded with petrol bombs; Catholic churches were attacked and burned because they were arsenals and priests handed out submachine guns to parishioners."*[77] Hardly a pastoral response, nor an accurate description of what happened.

Ultimately the man was an enigma. He had a lot of good: the apostolic conviction, the clarity, the desire to reach the lost, the organisational leadership, the counter-cultural lifestyle, all of which we can say we are sorely lacking in much of today's church. But he mixed it with some serious sectarianism, an uncontrolled tongue, and a lack of repentance on these issues, at least in word - though his 'Chuckle Brothers' friendship with Martin McGuinness showed that he had, in practice, mellowed.[78] If you're wondering how a true believer could have such a significant blindspot and such areas of inconsistency, just look at the anti-Semitic rants of Martin Luther in his later life if you're a Protestant, or if you're a Catholic and you hate Luther, take a quick look at the Spanish Inquisition. Or just look at your own life honestly.

In sum, the state of Protestant Christianity in Ulster has not been helped by the decades of very public, very open, very nasty, very deadly sectarianism which has sat alongside its doctrinal faithfulness. Just like how

---

[76] https://www.theguardian.com/politics/2014/sep/12/the-rev-ian-paisley
https://www.newsletter.co.uk/health/ian-paisley-received-800-letters-and-emails-catholic-constituents-praising-his-abortion-stance-2923315
Both accessed 16th December 2021
[77] https://www.bbc.co.uk/news/uk-northern-ireland-29171017 accessed 16th December 2021
[78] https://www.belfasttelegraph.co.uk/news/northern-ireland/how-martin-mcguinness-and-ian-paisley-forged-an-unlikely-friendship-35550640.html accessed 16th December 2021

Fifteens would decline in popularity if, alongside the marshmallows, cherries and coconut flakes, you decided to mix in a healthy dose of slurry to really stick it to the other side who aren't quite sure if they like Fifteens yet and are more committed to Caramel Squares at this point. There's good stuff in there somewhere, but the heavy layer of horse faeces doesn't do anyone any favours. Even if we remove the slurry and serve it up again, manure-free, sometimes it might take people a while to get over the aftertaste from their previous bite.

Perhaps if we had sought to reach our Catholic friends, demonstrated the gospel, and viewed them as either a mission field to be won or a group of errant brothers to be convinced, rather than as an enemy to be fought, then when Catholicism disintegrated in the '00s they would have come flocking to evangelicalism. We could have been in the greatest boom of Protestant Christianity anywhere in the Western World, with church growth and changed lives coming out of our ears on both sides of the border. Instead they abandoned Christianity entirely and ran to the welcoming arms, or rather vice-like grip, of secular leftism. It has become a modern-day trend to call Bible-believing Christians 'bigots' - a term normally unjustly flung around by those who ironically make up the least tolerant group on the planet. Unfortunately Northern Irish Protestantism's recent past has meant that there is far too much evidence for its truth when they direct it at us. Maybe we're reaping what we've sown.

Liberalism, lukewarmth and a leadership crisis

So where has all this left us? I can't really speak to the current state of the Catholic church, not being part of it, but when it comes to Northern Irish evangelicalism in the early 2020s, we're facing some major challenges.

The first of which would be rapidly encroaching theological liberalism. If the former generation made a mistake in mixing sectarianism in with Biblical faithfulness, the current generation is making the opposite mistake of mixing Biblical compromise in with non-sectarianism. Put off by the harsh dogmatism of former times that bore little spiritual fruit, we've assumed that the solution has been to relax our hold onto the truth of Scripture, rather than analyse our practice to make sure it is much closer to what the Bible actually says.

Much of this liberalisation has been couched in the language of mission and evangelism. We've been doing evangelism with a 'Christian-neutral world' mindset for quite some time, and in that world the most important elements of evangelism seemed to be respectability and kindness, or simply being nice. If we were thoughtful, sincere and welcoming to everyone, people would willingly listen to our position, and many would be convinced. We did, and many were convinced.

But times have changed. I'm not bashing niceness; gentleness, kindness, generosity, hospitality and love, rightly defined, are an essential part of the Christian witness. However we no longer live in that neutral world where demonstrating these attributes was enough to show people that you were 'nice' even if you disagreed with them on issues of sin and salvation. Now, in the Christian-negative world, the only way to be 'nice' is to agree. The changing idea of what tolerance is, from a willingness to live side-by-side with people who disagree to now ensuring that everyone must agree on every point or face the consequences, is a clear manifestation of this societal evolution. You must change your beliefs because those beliefs are the fundamental problem. Not agreeing is not nice, even if you do so with every ounce of Christian charity in your soul.

So Christians who found the heroin of respectability to be rather more-ish during the decades of neutrality are having a hard time getting clean in the age of negativity. Especially seeing as the change has been so rapid that the only option is to go cold turkey. Some can't hack it. The only solution for Christians whose very beliefs have now become the barrier to a good social image, and who want to maintain said image, is to compromise.

(I might add that it's fascinating that those who do so are the ones who major on themes like 'living like exiles' and so on, but who spend their time desperately trying to look like Babylonians. "Following Yahweh means being on the outside here in Babylon, and we should be willing to do so. On a totally unrelated note, however, have you tried worshipping the sun-god?")

There are two ways that I can see this liberalism occurring in Northern Irish Christianity, and broadly in the wider Christian world, at present. The first, and slightly rarer of the two, is outright denial of controversial Christian claims. It tends to be rarer at this point, at least in Northern Ireland, because the congregations are actually more Biblically faithful than many of the leadership, and if they pushed through the obvious denial of Scripture, their people would rightly leave. In other countries where this has been pushed through - Church of Scotland and Welsh Methodists, I'm looking at you here - the faithful congregations have already left, and so the leadership can go about merrily apostatising in front of their six remaining parishioners. Northern Ireland is not quite there yet. I met with a local pastor privately not long ago, and he has personally caved on both substitutionary atonement and the notion that hell has any eternal consequences - he reckons there's postmortem salvation, basically Rob Bell's 'Love Wins' position. As it was private, I won't out him by disclosing who it is. But aside from a vague reference that gave away his hand to anyone listening carefully, he hasn't preached on these issues publicly yet. I presume that's because his position is much more liberal than that of his flock.

Don't get me wrong, there are a reasonable number of church members who would quite enjoy a rapid liberal slide. John Alderdice, former leader of the Alliance Party, was spitting feathers when the Irish Presbyterians affirmed what they always believed about homosexuality, resigning his eldership and accusing them of changing to essentially become the Free P's.[79] I find that remarkable, seeing as he was part of the leadership of the Alliance Party in the early 1980s, a time when the Alliance Party did not support the mere decriminalisation of homosexuality in Northern Ireland.[80] So either in the 1980s John Alderdice was somehow theologically convinced that same-sex relationships were a-ok with God but at the same time thought they should be completely illegal - a remarkable

---

[79] https://www.belfasttelegraph.co.uk/news/northern-ireland/lord-alderdice-resigns-from-presbyterian-church-following-ban-on-same-sex-relationships-37011414.html accessed 16th December 2021
[80] https://www.libdems.org.uk/john_alderdice
https://www.belfasttelegraph.co.uk/news/northern-ireland/belfast-city-council-votes-in-favour-of-gay-marriage-31271172.html
Both accessed 16th December 2021

intellectual backflip - or he is the one who changed his position, not the Presbyterians.

The second, and definitely more common, form of liberalism occurring in Northern Irish Christianity is liberalism through silence. Sometimes this can be an intentional tactic to encourage liberalising, like emergent theologian Brian MacLaren's *'five-year moratorium'* on talking about gay relationships, before coming out firmly in favour thereof.[81] Other times, it's just cowardice. I know multiple Presbyterian congregants who, in spite of the denomination's official stance on the same-sex issue, sincerely believe that the church now thinks it's all ok because their minister hasn't said anything and 'times have changed'. Similarly a former church leader of mine said in private that we held to traditional Christian morality, but we would never say a word on it publicly. These are all wonderful examples of obedience to the most oft-repeated commandment in Scripture, "Be very afraid." Oh, wait, that's not it. How did it go again…?

My impression from much of the preaching in Northern Irish churches is that we've become accidental Pietists. By that I don't mean that we have become more pious or sincere, but that we've embraced a form of detachment from the world, like a sort of New Testament version of the Essenes, that refuses to meaningfully engage with culture. Our preaching has become therapeutic, primarily encouraging a healthy emotional state, private devotions, and a public life that essentially involves keeping one's nose clean and

---

[81] https://www.reform-magazine.co.uk/2015/01/brian-mclaren-interview-changing-faith-staying-faithful/
https://www.christianitytoday.com/news/2012/september/brian-mclaren-leads-commitment-ceremony-at-sons-same-sex.html
Both accessed 16th December 2021

innocuous pleasantness, but little more. That message has little to say to our current age, and thank goodness for that, because otherwise we could get into trouble.

This silent liberalisation has issues even for those who adopt it. Firstly, the world is decidedly *not* silent on these issues, but busy filling the discipleship vacuum that our silence has created. Older generations may have a degree of moral momentum that will carry them through to their graves, but young people do not, and our silence is setting them up for destruction down the line. Secondly, silence will not appease the world at all. The malevolent spirit of the age, this ravenous lion seeking to devour whoever it can, does not want little enclaves of people who disagree, even if they do not voice it. So if the aim of silence is to avoid persecution then that tactic has a very limited shelf-life. And thirdly, once you stop talking about something, you stop valuing it up, making your own liberalisation more likely. If you don't fight for something, chances are you will ultimately fight against it once the shooting starts.

The second major issue facing Northern Irish Christianity after liberalism is a general malaise of lukewarmth. (I know 'lukewarmth' is technically not a word, and I should really write 'lukewarmness', but my gosh, what an ugly and unnecessary word that is. You all understand lukewarmth perfectly and it sounds better, so I'm rolling with that.) Naturally lukewarmth is hard to measure precisely; when does a nice cup of tea become too cold to drink? You only really know for sure whenever you take a sip and have to spit it back into the cup. The signs are there that we're close to this point.

To start with, in an attempt to rid ourselves of the overly formulaic, routine-oriented, outward-appearance-of-godliness Christianity of our past, we've decided that the best option is to remove any sense of diligence, discipline or distinctiveness from our Christian lives. Sure, Ian Paisley may have overstated things when he said that all dancing was sinful, but that doesn't mean that Jesus is a big fan of his followers drunkenly twerking on strangers 'in da club'.[82] Whether we're in the 2020s or not, that doesn't change the fact that twerking is for the marriage bedroom only, and should be done sober so you remember the enjoyable experience.

Of course I'm not suggesting that provocative dancing is the cause of Christianity's downfall. Rather, that we have simply embraced the spirit of the world into the church, refused to call sin 'sin', and failed to encourage a holy lifestyle among God's people.

Again, our preaching is at fault here. To the lost, we have preached a gospel that sounds much more like, "If you're hurting, come to Jesus for healing," but leaves out, "If you're sinful, come to Jesus for forgiveness." And to the church, rather than saying anything resembling John Owen's commanding dictum, *"Be killing sin, or sin will be killing you,"* we have rather proclaimed, "Make peace with sin, and you'll probably be fine, because, like, Jesus is the answer. Oh, and there's free cookies at the back."[83] Powerful stuff.

Multiple things signal this dip in the temperature of modern Christianity. Those who consider themselves committed church members, rather than attending weekly services, now attend roughly monthly. Trips away, brunches, kids' activities and a general broader

---

[82] https://www.bbc.co.uk/news/uk-northern-ireland-29171017 accessed 16th December 2021
[83] John Owen, Terry Kulakowski, *Mortification of Sin* (Reformed Church Publications, 2015, originally published 1656) page 17

culture of low commitment means other things take priority over gathering with the body.[84] That's not to mention the impact of Covid and the idea that people can 'attend' online at a time and place of their choosing. Of course, this comes back to a lack of understanding as to what church is - a family and an army - neither of which function without serious commitment, meaningful discipline, and either in-person gatherings or in-person warfare. Such a lack of investment shows we don't know what the church really is, or what it's for.

Prayer has diminished in the Northern Irish church. It is not only my recollection, but that of multiple church leaders I have spoken with, that the 90s and 00s were a time of relentless, round-the-clock prayer, and the 24/7 prayer movement was at its peak in our country.[85] In my teen years during the 00s, I recall there being a genuine expectation of revival, with people stirred up to intense intercession for the province. Once again, the perception of everyone I've spoken with on the topic is that this has waned.[86] It's hard to know why; perhaps our expectations of revival were not fulfilled, and we became discouraged. However we got here, we have arrived at a place of lukewarm prayer.

Finally, Covid has been an apocalyptic event for the church in the truest sense of the word ('apocalypse' literally means 'unveiling'). Since the first lockdowns, one in three practising Christians have stopped attending church either in-person or online.[87] A further 34% have been regularly tuning into another church

---

[84] https://careynieuwhof.com/10-reasons-even-committed-church-attenders-attending-less-often/ accessed 16th December 2021
[85] https://renewaljournal.com/2019/09/18/the-amazing-journey-of-24-7-prayer/ accessed 9th December 2021
[86] https://www.premierchristianity.com/home/terry-virgo-whatever-happened-to-the-promised-revival/3096.article accessed 9th December 2021
[87] https://www.barna.com/research/new-sunday-morning-part-2/ accessed 16th December 2021

apart from their own.[88] And whilst 74% of Boomers (born 1946-1964) and 65% of Gen X-ers (born 1965-1981) have continued going to church, half of Millennials (born 1982-1996) have stopped going entirely.[89] Since returning to in-person services, the Evangelical Alliance in the UK reports that attendance has dropped by 32%.[90] And that assumes that we think online-only church is equally as valid as in-person gathering. Returning to my family-army analogy from above, there will never be Zoom-only childrearing or a successful military invasion by Skype. Covid has broken habitual Christianity and shown the true temperature of many professing believers.

Our final major issue in the Northern Irish church is that we are in the midst of a full-blown leadership crisis. I'll be quick with this one, because it doesn't take much explanation. If you look around the province's leading churches, both numerically and in terms of influence, you can easily see that the state of leadership in the church has fallen significantly over the last decade or so.

Ian Paisley, founder of the Free Presbyterian Church, James McConnell of Whitewell Metropolitan Tabernacle, and James Connolly of Glenmachan Church of God - all widely known church leaders in the province - have all passed away in recent years.[91] Paul and Priscilla Reid of CFC Belfast stepped aside from their leadership role in 2011, and their successor Andrew

---

[88] Ibid
[89] Ibid
[90] https://www.facebook.com/evangelicalalliance/photos/pcb.4637756146291614/4637753539625208 accessed 16th December 2021
[91] https://www.bbc.co.uk/news/uk-northern-ireland-29177705
https://www.bbc.co.uk/news/uk-northern-ireland-57873316
https://www.funeraltimes.com/lilyconnolly465590261
All accessed 16th December 2021

McCourt left for Sacramento, California in 2015.[92] Alan Scott, founder of Causeway Coast Vineyard, also stepped down and left for California in 2017.[93] (Can I just add that I hope climate change turns California into Arctic tundra?) Other notable church leaders like Derek McKelvey of Fisherwick Presbyterian and John Dickinson of Carnmoney Presbyterian have also retired in the last few years.[94] I obviously don't expect everyone to agree with everything the names on this list has ever said; they don't all agree with each other. But we *can* all agree that they were among the most influential church leaders in their various spheres of Northern Irish Christianity, that they have since left those roles in one way or another, and that their replacement has been a significant challenge.

This leadership crisis goes further, but time does not permit me to go into detail about the recent high-profile scandals involving other notable church leaders, or the fact that the Presbyterian church has barely anyone applying for church leadership roles or attending Union College.[95] We are in a state of genuine emergency, and though its effects may not have been fully felt yet, they are looming. Combined with our liberalism and our lukewarmth, we find the Northern Irish church of today in need of a serious awakening if our province is to be saved from calamity.

---

[92] https://cornerstonecity.church/paul-reid
https://www.youtube.com/watch?v=8Pi-ks7EuuY
Both accessed 16th December 2021
[93] https://www.charismanews.com/world/75087-how-a-move-of-god-in-northern-ireland-provides-the-blueprint-for-reclaiming-cities accessed 16th December 2021
[94] https://www.linkedin.com/in/derek-mckelvey-11a39a1b?originalSubdomain=uk
https://www.newtownabbeytoday.co.uk/news/people/carnmoney-minister-retires-after-19-years-3100334
Both accessed 16th December 2021
[95] https://www.belfasttelegraph.co.uk/opinion/columnists/alf-mccreary/churches-need-to-ponder-why-the-decline-in-attendance-is-so-severe-35882443.html accessed 16th December 2021

Taking responsibility

One thing I've seen with remarkable regularity over the last decade or so is believers and church leaders celebrating the death of the Christian culture in the West.[96] Those doing so tend to emphasise the potential upsides of such a societal change: an end to nominal faith with only the sincere believers remaining, a refining of the church, and new opportunities for evangelism. In one sense, I agree; God will use this for those purposes and then some.

However there is a vast difference between saying that something can be used for good by God and that the thing is good in itself. God can use a family breakup, a cancer diagnosis, or a funeral to bring people to Himself, but that doesn't mean divorce, disease or death are themselves positive. We don't celebrate when someone tells us they're going through any of those things; to do so would be not only inappropriate, but a violation of God's revealed nature and His instructions to the church. Similarly, celebrating the end of Christian culture is an act of gross ignorance.

Let me be clear: the disintegration of Christian society is absolutely terrible. There are a few reasons for this, the first of which being that we will now enter a society governed by moral norms that come from somewhere other than Scripture, and which are far worse than what we currently have. Christianity has produced the greatest societies in the history of the world - not that they have been by any means flawless - but they have had a greater respect for human life, personal liberty, private property and the wellbeing of the vulnerable

---

[96] https://www.christianitytoday.com/ct/podcasts/quick-to-listen/future-of-christianity.html accessed 16th December 2021

than anywhere else on earth. All of these values derive from the Bible, and cannot be consistently worked out from secularism, Islam, communism, wokeism or any other worldview. There is no neutral ground, all societies are fundamentally religious, and Christianity is not only the best one but also the only true one. If you thought sectarianism was bad, just imagine a world without the Bible as an ultimate standard to appeal to that can correct it. A society that abandons Christianity will embrace something worse, and if we continue to do so, we will likely enter a period of violence, economic contraction and social decay.

It's also terrible for the nation because it brings about the judgement of God. I know we don't like to think in these terms, but the reality is that God both raises up nations and casts them down. Try reading the Bible cover to cover, Genesis to Revelation, and come to any other conclusion. We see clearly from passages like Deuteronomy 28, Leviticus 26 and Revelation 11 that God holds nations accountable for the light that they have received. Furthermore Jesus wept over Jerusalem because He ministered among them for three years and they rejected Him. He knew that they would be destroyed for doing so; something which happened forty years after His ascension when the city was razed to the ground and its inhabitants slaughtered by the Romans in 70AD. Sure, God used their rejection of Christ to save the entire world, but it didn't make that rejection any more commendable or worthy of celebration, and it ended in bloody deaths for those who did so. Likewise, we have had plenty and we have rejected it. We should look at our nation, see what is coming if we continue down this path, and weep. Anything other than this shows an astounding lack of compassion towards our people.

Finally, it's terrible because such a collapse is literally a damning indictment against the church. It is God and the world saying, "There is no flavour in this salt, it is fit only to be trampled underfoot." Remember how we started this chapter? We are responsible for the direction of our culture. By any meaningful standard, it seems we have failed. The blame for nominal Christianity, so historically present in the Western world, cannot be laid at the feet of the culture, but at the feet of the church. We have allowed this. We have preached a soft gospel. We have refused to discipline the sins that are socially acceptable, from sectarianism to sexual immorality. We have loved the world, which is enmity with God. We have spoken peace where there is no peace. It's on us. The primary issue is not the sin out in the world, it is the sin in the church. Should we celebrate the revelation of our spiritual poverty? No, we should repent.

Fortunately God loves repentance. And in the next chapter, we'll see the great things He has done in our nation when the church has truly sought Him.

Discussion Questions

1 – Have you noticed the decline of the Northern Irish church, and if so, in what ways?

2 – Seeing as that decline has taken place, what areas of society do you think have been most impacted by that decline, and what are you most passionate to see turned around?

3 – What are you going to do about either of the above two questions?

4 – What signs of life do you see in Northern Irish Christianity?

CHAPTER 4
KEEP 'ER LIT
Or: The Legacy Of Past Irish Revivals

So back in the day, some people I'm friends with were planting a church and were looking for a meeting venue. They had found a potential building in the approximate area they were looking for, down in inner East Belfast, and asked me to come along and have a look at it with them. They never said exactly why they asked me, however I'm sure that my extensive experience of having lived in several buildings and having been inside many more over the course of my lifetime, made me an excellent candidate. I, with all my expertise in tow, duly obliged.

So I went to check it out along with one of the team, let's call her Lucy. For reasons that will become apparent later in the story, I'll tell you now that her background is much more working class than mine. It was a little community centre with a large enough hall for a moderate church gathering, a functioning kitchen, and some space upstairs for kids work, all nicely done up and with a lovely manager. At the end of looking around, the manager asked us would we like to see the war museum on the third floor.

"Oh yes, sounds great!" I said, sincerely interested. We only had a few minutes, but I wouldn't have thought a community-run place like this would have a museum, and loved the idea of bringing some extra-curricular history to young people. So, up we went.

And it was actually really high quality. This medium-sized room, say about thirty square metres, was chock full of military history from Northern Irish soldiers in the British army. There were uniforms, lots of old artefacts, black-and-white pictures, panels with intriguing vignettes, all centred around the young men of east Belfast who had volunteered and served their country. For a wee community centre, it was really well done. Lucy seemed slightly more reserved than I was, but I decided to be genuinely effusive in my praise for the both of us as we looked around.

"This is class." "Where did you get all this stuff from?" "I'll come back when I have more time to have a proper look around." "It's great to commemorate this kind of sacrifice." And so on.

We had a quick discussion about hiring terms and left shortly after. As we were walking out, I said to Lucy, "That was really good, wasn't it?" She turned to me and replied, "You do realise that was a full on UVF promotional display, don't you?" Ah. Funyuns. I had not.

In my defence, I had a very sheltered upbringing that involved minimal exposure to paramilitaries other than in name, and they didn't exactly have it spray-painted on the wall as I would have expected. But before anyone digs into my past and has me cancelled, I would like to get ahead of the game and offer a full, public apology for my vigorous-though-unwitting support of Loyalist terrorism.

Heritage is an interesting thing though. It's amazing how a group of people can take something that is very tangled, messy, and in this case destructive, and yet trace the roots of it back to their beginning, and honour that past. To be fair, the original UVF legitimately fought and died in great number in the Battle of the Somme, although the modern organisation bears no actual connection to the historical one, other than using the same name and logo.[97] In Northern Ireland both sides of the Protestant-Catholic divide have made a big deal about their history and culture, and rightly so. Understanding your history helps you understand today, and in many ways can give a glimpse into the future.

One place that has done little to honour its heritage, however, is the modern evangelical church. We often imagine that we have arrived at the pinnacle of Christian knowledge and understanding, having nothing to gain by honouring our spiritual fathers and mothers through giving them a fair hearing - something C.S. Lewis called 'chronological snobbery'.[98] This is deeply sad, because the history of the church on this island is an astounding story of spiritual warfare, daring escapades, and God's power to transform the world from just about anywhere. Yet most of us younger evangelicals live completely detached from our past, and don't bother looking there for ideas as to what God might want to do today.

This is, in my opinion, actually a sin issue. Over and over again in Scripture, the people of God are called to

---

[97] https://www.irishnews.com/news/2016/06/30/news/the-somme---ulster-unionism-s-blood-sacrifice-584061/
https://www.bbc.co.uk/news/uk-northern-ireland-22229750
Both accessed 16th December 2021
[98] C.S. Lewis, *Surprised By Joy* (William Collins, 2010, first published 1955) page 241

remember what He has done for them. The Passover was a call to remember God's deliverance from Egypt; Deuteronomy gives an entire list of Israel's journey to the Promised Land and calls them to remember, warning them not to forget; Judges, Psalms and Isaiah all tell us that one of the causes of the sin of the nation was that they did not remember what God had done for them; Purim was instituted as a feast to remember the deliverance God worked through Esther; David tells us that he both remembers and even meditates on what God did in history; the church is called to remember what we have received and heard, and importantly for this chapter, from where we have fallen; and Jesus tells us to take communion in remembrance of Him.[99] This isn't just some triviality. A people who forget what God has done will ultimately also forget what He commands.

Some might argue that this really only applies to Scripture and God's works there. I agree that that is the primary focus of these texts, but I also think we can see an overarching principle at work. For instance, no one would argue against it being spiritually necessary to remember God's work in your own life. If you never recall how He has saved you, led you, provided for you or done miracles for you, you are missing a significant part of what you can thank God for and learn from. To forget this would be sheer spiritual negligence. Likewise, why would it be anything other than helpful and important to learn the history of what God has done in our nation?

There's also the fact that God remembers. Without doing a similar listing of texts, you can see over and over

---

[99] Exodus 12:14, Deuteronomy 8, Judges 8:34, Psalm 78:42, Isaiah 17:10, Psalm 143:5, Revelation 3:3, Revelation 2:5, Luke 22:19

again in Scripture that God remembers what He has done, and that we are called to ask Him to do it again. In fact one of the great patterns of Scripture is that the future often reflects the past, as God teases His plans in advance and then works them out in full down the road.

Alongside this, I'm also a firm believer that God, as well as dealing with churches as individual congregations, entire denominations and throughout the entire wider world at any time, also deals with churches in geographical groups. For further details, see the letters to the seven Asian churches in Revelation 1-3, the *'grace given to the Macedonian churches'*, or Paul's introduction to Galatians.[100] God relates to churches in localities, recalls what He has done for them and through them, and has collective plans for them.

All that to say, if we want a fresh revival on this island, we would do well to know something about its revivals of old. As I alluded to earlier, we should remember the height from which we have fallen, and try to get back there. Our spiritual heritage not only provides encouragement from history, it also tells us how we must use the birthright given to us by our godly ancestors today, and it shows us how God might want to use us in the future. By the way, if that's the case, then it's absolutely awesome; our national church history involves the salvation of the Western world the last time civilisation collapsed. Maybe this time, seeing as it's all falling apart again, our role will look something like that. But how can we possibly know our national divine destiny without knowing our national divine history?

So, anyone fancy some cool revival stories? Brilliant, that's what this chapter is about. Let's get stuck in.

---

[100] Revelation 1:3, 2 Corinthians 8:1, Galatians 1:2

Saint Paddy

The Roman Empire didn't technically fall overnight, but compared to both its scale and longevity, it might as well have. Founded as a Republic in central Italy in 509BC, it grew to dominate the Mediterranean and Western Europe by the time it became an Empire four hundred and eighty years later.[101] From there, it expanded further to stretch from Scotland to Saudi Arabia at its peak. Its downfall didn't hit in earnest until around the late AD300s, almost eight centuries after its founding.[102] To put that into context, the United States didn't exist until around two hundred and fifty years ago, and didn't become the world's undisputed leading economic power until around 1900, just over a century ago.[103]

In a series of events that will sound eerily familiar to modern Western readers, Rome fell apart in a mere couple of generations. Cultural decadence, political division, porous borders, mass immigration, incompetent leaders, economic mismanagement, over-taxation and a weakened military meant that Rome could no longer control much of its supposed territory, and the capital itself was sacked by the Visigoths in 410AD.[104] Over the coming century, the empire would functionally cease to exist.

The fall of Rome presented a great threat to Christianity, which was in many ways quite dependent

---

[101] https://www.britannica.com/place/Roman-Republic accessed 16th December 2021
[102] https://www.britannica.com/place/Roman-Empire accessed 16th December 2021
[103] https://world101.cfr.org/historical-context/world-war/how-did-united-states-become-global-power accessed 16th December 2021
[104] In general, Thomas Cahill, *How The Irish Saved Civilization* (Hodder and Staughton, 1995) page 9-31
Further details:
Jerry Toner, *Decadence And Literature* (Cambridge University Press, 2019) pages 15-29
David Gwynn, *A.H.M. Jones and the Later Roman Empire* (Brill, 2008) page 237
Bryan Ward-Perkins, *The Fall Of Rome* (OUP Oxford, 2006) page 68
Sam Moorehead, David Stuttard, *AD410* (J Paul Getty Museum, 2010) page 16

upon the Roman state and infrastructure. The barbarians, now invading various cities with regularity, sought to destroy Roman culture and its Greek foundations by burning libraries, smashing sculptures and destroying books. Twelve centuries of learning, including much Christian literature was under serious threat, and a huge portion was entirely lost.[105] Civilisation as everyone had come to know it had ended, and the church might well have gone with it.

But God had other plans. Ireland, detached from mainland Europe and full of violent clans, hadn't even been a target of Roman imperialism. We weren't worth the effort. One Roman geographer described us as, *"a people wanting in every virtue, and totally destitute of piety."* Cheers mate. But it was a fair description; indeed Irish pirates were a significant part of the threat to the ailing Roman Empire, and considered the fiercest tribe in the slavery business.[106] It was a dark, dangerous, nasty, immoral place. There were 'trial marriages' to allow men to have sex with whomever they pleased, and 'homosexual relations among warriors on campaign were more or less the order of the day'.[107] One clan inaugurated its kings through public copulation with a white mare.[108] That's not to mention the killing, with its druid leaders sacrificing newborns to the harvest gods and its warriors, who fought naked, using decapitated heads as cups and footballs.[109] Taranis, one of the three most significant Celtic gods, liked his victims burned in wicker baskets, whilst Esus, another one of them,

---

[105] Cahill, *How The Irish Saved Civilization*, page 58
[106] Ibid, page 37
[107] Ibid, 135
[108] Ibid, 135
[109] Ibid, 136

preferred his to be hanged or impaled.[110] If Satan ran a country, it would probably look like ancient Ireland.

But if that was the case, then the devil made a mistake. In 401AD, right around the time the Visigoths first attacked Italy, Irish pirates kidnapped a young British teenager called Patricius, today known as Patrick.[111]

Though Patrick had grown up in a Christian context, he had mocked priests and paid little attention to religion. But upon being suddenly ripped from his home by savage foreigners and forced into hungry, frigid work as a shepherd in the wilds of Antrim, he believed he was being judged by God, and began to pray.[112] He wrote, *"I would pray constantly during the daylight hours. The love of God and the fear of Him surrounded me more and more... In one day I would say as many as a hundred prayers and after dark nearly the same again..."*[113]

After six years of slavery and isolation, suddenly a voice spoke to him in the night, saying *"Your hungers are rewarded: you are going home."* As he sat up, startled, the voice continued, *"Look, your ship is ready."*[114]

Taking this to be a word from God, Patrick set out into the wilderness for an unknown port, and walked, led by the Spirit, for two hundred miles over strange territory, until he finally saw his ship, likely somewhere near Wexford.[115] He went up to the sailors, aware he looked a lot like a runaway slave, and asked to board. They said no, so he walked off and prayed, during which one of

---

[110] John Haywood, *The Celts* (Taylor & Francis, 2014) page 43
and also https://anchor.fm/the-theology-pugcast/episodes/The-Irish-Saints-Redeemed-Paganism-eu7tfu - minutes 7-8, accessed 9 December 2021
[111] Ibid, 39
Also https://www.jstor.org/stable/3296883 accessed 16th December 2021
[112] Cahill, *How The Irish Saved Civilization*, page 102
Confession of St Patrick 1.
[113] Cahill, *How The Irish Saved Civilization*, page 102
[114] Ibid, 103
[115] Ibid, 103

them ran after him saying they had changed their mind. In keeping with some rather disgusting custom, they offered their nipples to be sucked as a sign of good faith. Patrick, allegedly due to religious conviction, declined. Fortunately they let him on anyway, perhaps with a sense of disappointment on their part, but almost certainly with sense of relief for Patrick.[116] They took him with them to Europe, and after a few more years of travel he finally arrived back home to his family in Britain.[117]

But Patrick, transformed by his years of hard labour and prayer, could no longer play the part of a Roman teenager. He was restless. One night he had a vision in which Victoricus, a man he knew from Ireland, appeared to him, handing him countless letters with the heading *Vox Hibernionacum - The Voice Of The Irish*.[118] The moment he saw those words, he heard the voice of a countless multitude crying out, *"We beg you, holy youth, that you shall come and shall walk again among us."*[119] Sensing the call to be a missionary in Ireland, he applied and was accepted for theological training in Gaul, before being ordained as probably the first missionary-bishop since the Apostle Paul.[120] In fact, considering the mission-fields up until that time had been within the Roman Empire, Patrick was arguably the first ever missionary into the brutal and uncivilised world. It was daring, pioneering stuff. As historian Thomas Cahill puts it, *"The step he took was every bit as bold as Columbus's,"* or as Patrick in his own words wrote, *"every day I am ready to be murdered, betrayed, enslaved—*

---

[116] Ibid, 103-104
[117] Ibid, 105
[118] Ibid, 105
[119] Confession of St Patrick, 23.
[120] Cahill, *How The Irish Saved Civilization*, page 106-107

whatever may come my way. But I am not afraid of any of these things, because of the promises of heaven; for I have put myself in the hands of God Almighty."[121] His courage set the tone for the later Irish fearless missionary zeal.

Thus he embarked on a thirty-year mission to Ireland, where he stayed for the rest of his life, and transformed the nation.

St Patrick's success came down to a few key things. Firstly, he wholeheartedly embraced the Irish people as his own, becoming an adopted Irishman himself, and identifying with them far more than with his Roman-British background.[122] For instance, he spoke in glowing terms about *"a blessed woman, Irish by birth, noble, extraordinary, beautiful - a true adult - whom I baptised"* - a kind of warmth unheard of in that era, particularly when said of a woman. At the same time he openly confronted his British overseers who did not view the Irish Christians as fully saved or fully human.[123] Furthermore his authoritative stance against slavery, publicly condemning it with terms like *'a crime so horrible and unspeakable'* on a regular basis, demonstrated his true care for the lowest classes of Irish society.[124] Cahill writes that Patrick was *"the first human in the history of the world to speak out unequivocally against slavery. Nor will any voice as strong as his be heard again till the seventeenth century."*[125]

Secondly, he was recklessly courageous, not only in coming to Ireland, but in his activity once he arrived. His methods involved direct confrontation with the druid leadership, demonstrating the truth of his message over

---

[121] Ibid, 108
[122] Ibid, 109-110
[123] Ibid, 109-112
[124] Ibid, 110-114
[125] Ibid, 114

and against theirs, in a way that these ferocious occultists were unlikely to take lying down. One story speaks of his actions at the Hill of Tara, where an annual pagan festival was to be celebrated. According to the custom, no one was allowed to light a fire until the High King, Laeghairé, first lit his ceremonial flame on top of that hill. Patrick decided the appropriate thing to do was to go up the Hill of Slane, just across the way, and start his Easter fire a bit early. Needless the say, the priest-king was not best pleased, and sent twenty-seven chariots across to go fetch Patrick. As they came, he shouted out to them the words of Psalm 20:7: "*Some trust in chariots and some in horses, but we trust in the name of the LORD our God.*" They failed to capture him, and amazingly Patrick's courage instead won him an audience with the High King the following day, who then granted him permission to preach the gospel across Ireland.[126] This refusal to be afraid demonstrated a sanctified version of the courage that the Irish believed to be a virtue, and won the hearts of many.[127]

Miracles were a common occurrence in Patrick's ministry, and were doubtless an essential catalyst for demonstrating the reality of his message. Though the idea that he literally drove snakes out of the island is historically unsupported, this idea likely stemming from the spiritual deliverance of the nation from innumerable forms of darkness during his ministry, there are many stories that bear the ring of truth. It appears that he survived attempts at poisoning by praying over the contaminated food and was entirely unharmed.[128]

---

[126] Joseph Sanderson, *The Story of Saint Patrick* (Richardson, 1895) page 128-131
[127] Cahill, *How The Irish Saved Civilization*, page 124
[128] Mary Francis Cusack, William Maunsell Hennessy, *The Life of Saint Patrick, Apostle of Ireland* (Catholic Pub Soc, 1869) page 259

Another account speaks of him confronting a druid magician, Lochru, who attacked Patricks' teaching, but was then snatched up into the air by an invisible force as Patrick prayed, and dropped to his death. On another occasion, we are told that his enemies were scattered in supernatural confusion like those sent to arrest Elisha in 2 Kings 6, as they set upon Patrick to kill him.[129] Most convincing of all to me are the testimonies of extraordinary healing miracles such as blind eyes opening and the mute speaking were a regular occurrence, with as many as thirty-three people raised from the dead through his ministry.[130] Secular historians - and probably a few cessationists - try and explain away these miracles as products of legend, but any reasonable person would have a hard time explaining the radical transformation of a nation in such short time without such wonder-working power.

He was also a strategist and leader. Ireland lacked population centres of note, so he went about training and appointing bishops across the island. His tactic was to spread them across the territory, doing so successfully in every province, though the far west remained a remote and difficult place to crack.[131] And due to the lack of major cities, he placed them within spitting distance of the capitals of the various rulers and tribal kings, as well as near the high king in Tara, so that they could speak to the ruling powers and be present at the key gathering points for what was otherwise a scattered, rural population.[132] This wise strategy meant that the gospel influenced the whole nation, top to bottom.

---

[129] Ibid, page 256
[130] William Bullen Morris, *The Life of Saint Patrick, Apostle of Ireland* (Burns and Oates, 1878) page 147
[131] Gribben, *The Rise And Fall Of Christian Ireland*, page 35
[132] Cahill, *How The Irish Saved Civilization*, page 109-110

Finally, his preaching was a direct attack on the evil Celtic deities, demonstrating the overwhelming power and goodness of the God of Scripture. Instead of trick-working, malevolent gods, who could shape-shift into various natural objects but were themselves also mere parts of creation, Patrick preached a God who made everything out of nothing, who made it good, and who entered His creation in the Incarnation to rescue mankind.[133] Rather than a panoply of gods with competing interests and motives, he preached a unified, Trinitarian God who was three-yet-one, embodying perfect love.[134] And in place of bloodthirsty deities who demanded their subjects sacrifice their own sons, he taught a God who gave His own Son as the once-for-all sacrifice for sins, granting us the free gift of eternal life in the process.[135] His message was not just generic good news, but specific good news for these people, living under these conditions, speaking to their spiritual hunger.

Patrick's ministry had a profound effect on the island. It's believed that Patrick's ministry led to the planting of three hundred churches across Ireland, and 120,000 converts baptised.[136] Considering that the total population of the island was likely around half a million at the time, all completely unreached and enthusiastically pagan, that's an astonishing harvest.[137] Not bad for a runaway slave. And his impact didn't stop there. By the end of his life, slavery and human sacrifice had become unthinkable on the island, and warfare

---

[133] Gribben, Crawford, *The Rise And Fall Of Christian Ireland* (Oxford University Press, 2021) page 33
[134] St Patrick's Breastplate - see https://www.irishcentral.com/roots/st-patricks-breastplate-prayer-irelands-patron-saint accessed 16th December 2021
[135] Ibid, 140-141
[136] Gordon Pettie, *Do It Again Lord*, page 50
[137] https://forum.paradoxplaza.com/forum/threads/irish-population-history-my-estimates.1182719/ accessed 16th December 2021

between the tribes, though impossible to eradicate entirely, had greatly decreased.[138] Furthermore, Ireland became unique as a land into which Christianity was introduced without the bloodshed of its followers - there were very few Irish martyrs for their faith. And just to draw this all back to Northern Ireland, his ministry had both a focus upon and arguably its largest impact in Ulster.[139] After all, he's buried here in Downpatrick - so there.[140]

It was the Christianisation of Ireland that made it a haven for both Christian and other classical literature and education; a place where books and Scriptures were sent for protection, reading and transcribing, and where church leaders were trained en masse, and a base for missions.[141] As the death of the surrounding world coincided with the birth of a godly nation, this remote island went from being a barbarous, pagan place to the global hub of Christianity in the blink of an eye. Both spiritually devout and intellectually gifted, Ireland was now 'the land of saints and scholars'.

The next mission? Win back the world for Jesus.

Saints, scholars and savage missionaries

One thing I didn't mention about the druids earlier was that these guys were not idiots. You might think that they had barely two braincells to rub between them, what with their violence and mysticism, but that couldn't be further from the truth. Druids were profoundly well educated, often studying for twenty

---

[138] Cahill, *How The Irish Saved Civilization*, page 148, 110
[139] Ibid
[140] https://discovernorthernireland.com/things-to-do/down-cathedral-and-saint-patricks-grave-p675961 accessed 16th December 2021
[141] Cahill, *How The Irish Saved Civilization*, page 151

years before being commissioned into their priestly role, a process that involved recalling the entire culture, law and history of the Irish from memory in what was an entirely oral culture.[142] Many of these druids were saved under Patrick's ministry, and this deep commitment to learning and history had made the Irish pagan leaders the perfect people to preserve and propagate Christian truth in the Western world, right as it crumbled everywhere else.[143] These men threw themselves into studying Christianity with the same stringent discipline they had used for paganism, learning Greek, Hebrew and Latin, memorising Scripture, developing their own written language, and even making literacy more accessible by inventing things like spaces between words and basic punctuation, neither of which existed at the time.[144] Modern Western readers may be tempted to think, "Ancient languages and literary scholarship – snooze." but it was the most important thing happening in the world at the time.

By the early 500s, it was evident that Irish paganism was a spent force, and the Irish church began to both consolidate and move forwards. Using the clan structure like a battle map, monasteries were established in strategic locations across the island.[145] Now don't think that Irish monasticism was a way for devout people with strange haircuts to get away from the corrupting influence of society. Not at all. Irish monasteries were often placed at the centres of civilisation and became the focal point of clan life. Clonmacnoise, for instance, was placed at the major crossroads of the only east-west land

---

[142] https://anchor.fm/the-theology-pugcast/episodes/The-Irish-Saints-Redeemed-Paganism-eu7tfu - accessed 9 December 2021
[143] Ibid
[144] Ibid
[145] Gribben, *The Rise And Fall Of Christian Ireland* page 37

route through the bogs of central Ireland and the busy River Shannon, not only a strategic location, but as it was in the very centre of the island it also stood as an implicit declaration that all Ireland belonged to Jesus.[146] Detachment from the church in Rome meant that Irish monks were often married, and rather than being a place of escapism, Irish monasteries *"became the laboratories of an energetic and often daring Christian culture."*[147] Less like quiet centres of contemplation, these were more like buzzing hives of family, business, trade, education, art and information, as well as Bible teaching and prayer. Think of them as some sort of mash-up between a home, a church, a school, a university, a factory, a Bible college, a media centre, a music studio and an art gallery, all with Christ as their Head.[148] These were not places of retreat, they were places of advance.

(NB - it's worth adding that Protestants need not worry here; though the later practices of many monasteries were legalistic in the extreme, these started out as centres of true Christian faith.)

Finnian of Clonard (470-549AD) was arguably the most important of these monks, though he's not the most famous. The famous ones were all part of a group twelve major figures after Patrick, collectively known as the twelve apostles of Ireland. Finnian taught all of them.[149] Not that it was just them, at any one time Finnian's monastery may have had as many as three thousand students - making it one of the most remarkable educational institutes in the world at the

---

[146] https://www.visitoffaly.ie/Places-to-Go/Clonmacnoise-Monastic-Site/ accessed 9 December 2021
[146] https://anchor.fm/the-theology-pugcast/episodes/The-Irish-Saints-Redeemed-Paganism-eu7tfu - accessed 9 December 2021
[147] Ibid, pages 39-40
[148] Ibid, 40-56
Cahill, *How The Irish Saved Civilization*, page 147-196
[149] https://www.yourirish.com/history/christianity/st-finnian-of-clonard accessed 13th December 2021

time.[150] No wonder; he was twice led by angels to start it, one angelic visitation telling him to return to Ireland from Wales, and another directing him where to set up his monastery.[151] And unlike modern monasteries, once Finnian considered a student's training to be complete, he would kick them out and get them to start their own.[152]

Ciarán of Clonmacnoise was one of the twelve. As a young man studying under Finnian, Ciarán had a copy of the gospel of Matthew which he leant to a friend. When being quizzed on the topic, his fellow students laughed at him because he had only memorised half of it, and nicknamed him 'Ciarán half-Matthew'. (Note the standard. Gulp!) Finnian, recognising the call of God on the young man, said to them, *"Not 'Ciarán half-Matthew', but 'Ciarán half-Ireland', for he will have half the country and the rest of us will have the other half."*[153]

Whilst on the islands of Aran, he and another monk called Enda both had the same vision of a great, beautiful tree on the banks of a stream in central Ireland, one which sheltered the nation, and the fruit of which went beyond the sea.[154] Enda explained the vision to Ciarán: *"The great tree is you, for you are great in the eyes of God and all people. All of Ireland will be sheltered by the grace in you, and many will be nourished by your fasting and prayers. Go to the centre of Ireland, and found your church on the banks of a stream."*[155] It was he who founded

---

[150] Thomas Moore *The History of Ireland by Thomas Moore* Volume 1 (Galilgnani, 1835) page 245
[151] https://stfinnian.webs.com/biography-of-st-finnian accessed 13th December 2021
[152] https://anchor.fm/the-theology-pugcast/episodes/The-Irish-Saints-Redeemed-Paganism-eu7tfu - accessed 9 December 2021
[153] https://www.oca.org/saints/lives/2014/09/09/102553-saint-ciaran-of-clonmacnoise accessed 13th December 2021
[154] John Monahan, *Records Relating to the Dioceses of Ardagh and Clonmacnoise* (1886) page 44
[155] https://www.irishcultureandcustoms.com/ASaints/Kieran.html accessed 16th December 2021

Clonmacnoise monastery at the great crossroads in the middle of Ireland.

Sadly Ciarán died within a year of founding the monastery. I say sadly; his fellow apostles were actually in one way happy about it, because they feared there would be no-one left to convert if he had stuck around much longer.[156] But his work was done and its impact was already guaranteed. His monastery went on to be arguably the greatest in Ireland, with half of the monasteries in the nation following the rule of Ciarán.[157]

When it comes to Ciarán's international influence, you may have some knowledge of Charlemagne, who led something of a cultural Renaissance in the AD800s. He essentially brought back a measure of literacy and learning that had disappeared after the fall of Rome. Charlemagne himself being illiterate, he employed someone to head all of this up and lead the University of Paris: an English monk called Alcuin of York. Alcuin was trained at Clonmacnoise.[158] Education returned to Europe because of someone trained at an Irish monastery.

Columcille, also known as Columba, was another of the twelve, and led the way for the Irish spiritual invasion of Britain.

Now to balance out all the stories of holiness and greatness, I should probably tell you how Columcille became a missionary. It wasn't by design. Columcille was a lover of beautiful books, and borrowed Finnian's copy of the Psalms, which was apparently extraordinarily beautiful, and highly valuable. He

---

[156] https://anchor.fm/the-theology-pugcast/episodes/The-Irish-Saints-Redeemed-Paganism-eu7tfu - accessed 9 December 2021
[157] https://www.britannica.com/biography/Saint-Ciaran-of-Clonmacnoise accessed 13th December
[158] Cahill, *How The Irish Saved Civilization*, pages 206-207

decided to make a copy, in secret, but was found out. Finnian was not pleased, and brought the case before King Diarmait, who ruled in Finnian's favour, declaring, "*To every cow her calf; to every book its copy.*" Cahill notes that this was the first copyright case in history.[159]

However, Columcille was not best pleased. Sometime later, Diarmait had one of Columcille's followers put to death, and so Columcille seized the chance to raise his clan for war with Diarmait's army. His clan won decisively, allegedly killing three thousand of the army and only losing one in the process. It may seem excessive, but did get his copy of the Psalms back, so there's that.[160] These guys may be great heroes of the faith, but they were still definitely Irish.

The monastic communities were firmly opposed to Columcille in this action and excommunicated him from the Irish church. Furthermore his penance, which if completed would allow him to return to the fold, was 'white martyrdom' - to sail off into the white of morning for the gospel.[161] (The Irish Christians felt bad that they weren't able to die for their faith in suitable numbers, so they coined the terms 'green martyrdom': becoming a monk - and 'white martyrdom': becoming a missionary, to make up for their lack of 'red martyrdom'.)[162] He was not allowed to return until he had converted more souls than had died in the battle he caused.[163]

Landing on Iona, Columcille and his friends built a few huts, some barns, some admin buildings, a library and a church, and they were ready for business – that was all they needed for their rhythm of study, prayer, farming

---

[159] Read the full story in Cahill. *How The Irish Saved Civilization*, pages 169-171
[160] Ibid
[161] Ibid, 184
[162] Ibid, 151
[163] Ibid, 171

and copying books[164] Visitors from all the surrounding tribes began to flood in, and many never left, not merely joining the faith but also the monastery.[165] Known today as the Apostle to the Picts, Columcille didn't want to merely build his own organisation, so he made one hundred and fifty monks the maximum permitted at Iona - any time they surpassed this, some were sent to found new monasteries and reach new regions.[166]

It was from Iona that another famous monastery, Lindisfarne, was launched in Northumbria. The Roman Britons had been somewhat Christianised prior to this time, but had been pushed back by tribes of Picts, Angles, Saxons and Jutes, who invaded from all sides. It took dauntless Celtic Christians to win back this territory for Christ. Cahill writes, *"As Columcille had baptized Scotland - and taught it to read - Aidan (the monk sent to set up Lindisfarne) would do the same for all of northern England."*[167] Columcille passed his three thousand souls with ease, and decided to keep going until he converted a couple of nations.

After Britain was continental Europe, and God's chosen instrument to get this started was Columbanus. Having trained at Bangor monastery - a place known for having hundreds of years of literally perpetual worship, the monks working in shifts to sing to God at all times - at the age of forty he began to hear the audible voice of God constantly telling him to preach the gospel in foreign lands.[168] After eventually getting permission to do so, Columbanus preached his way across France, and drew such a following that he needed a place to train his

---

[164] Ibid, 184
[165] Ibid, 184
[166] Ibid, 184-185
[167] Ibid, 187
[168] https://www.newadvent.org/cathen/04137a.htm accessed 13th December 2021

disciples. So, receiving use of a remote, dilapidated Roman fort, he set up a monastery in Annegray.[169] But his following continued to grow to the extent that he needed to start two more in the local area, one at Fontaines and one at Luxeuil.[170]

The European church at the time was corrupt and lax, whereas Columbanus' life was marked by strictness, austerity, boldness and no compromise.[171] He and his followers also had a kindness, humility and patience that was remarkable. And he could work miracles, healing a blind man at Orleans and the wife of his benefactor, and seeing several miracles around the multiplication and provision of food, including once during a famine.[172] Such things made him stand out and grew his popularity.

He moved with such speed that it inevitably annoyed the local bishops, who refused to leave their stately homes and travel anywhere so rough as Columbanus would for the sake of the gospel, their own comfort and safety taking priority. Jealous of his results, they summoned him to appear before them at a synod. Columbanus thought the whole thing was a waste of time, so sent a letter that very politely said something akin to, "Thank you so much for your invitation to look into this matter; it'd be great if you showed a similar concern for discernment regarding your own lives. Why

---

[169] Mike Bickle, *Growing In Prayer* (Charisma Media, 2014) page 244-245 and https://anchor.fm/the-theology-pugcast/episodes/The-Irish-Saints-Redeemed-Paganism-eu7tfu - accessed 9 December 2021
[170] Ibid
[171] https://anchor.fm/the-theology-pugcast/episodes/The-Irish-Saints-Redeemed-Paganism-eu7tfu - accessed 9 December 2021
[172] https://www.newadvent.org/cathen/04137a.htm
Jonas Of Bobbio, *The Life Of St Columban* (an old book, but this version was made available by the Department of History at University of Pennsylvania, 2007) page 32

not do your own jobs properly instead of criticising me for doing mine?"[173]

Though his wit and his willingness to fight got him in regular trouble, often being exiled for his stances, that didn't stop his success. If anything it further fuelled it: he took on the ungodly rulers across the nations, reprimanded the corrupt leadership in the church, assailed the Arian heretics, and even chastised the pope for his weak leadership.[174] In the process, he and his followers founded over one hundred monasteries, including some of the most essential education centres in Europe in the seventh and eighth centuries.[175] Furthermore, he functioned as the prototype for later Celtic and British missionaries to Europe, including Killian, Virgilius, Donatus, Wilfrid, Willibrord, Swithbert, and Boniface, who swept across the continent in the following generation.[176]

I can think of no better way to end this little subsection, or to summarise the boldness and impact of the Irish monks, than Cahill's synopsis:

"Monks began to set off in every direction, bent on glorious and heroic exile for the sake of Christ. They were warrior-monks, of course, and certainly not afraid of whatever monsters they might meet. Some went north, like Columcille. Others went northwest, like Brendan the Navigator, visiting Iceland, Greenland, and North America, and supping on the back of a whale in mid-ocean. Some set out in boats without oars, putting their

---

[173] Cahill, *How The Irish Saved Civilization*, pages 188-189
[174] https://anchor.fm/the-theology-pugcast/episodes/The-Irish-Saints-Redeemed-Paganism-eu7tfu - accessed 9 December 2021
[175] https://www.newadvent.org/cathen/04137a.htm accessed 16th December 2021
[176] https://www.newadvent.org/cathen/04137a.htm accessed 16th December 2021

destination completely in the hands of God. Many of the exiles found their way to continental Europe, where they were more than a match for the barbarians they met. They, whom the Romans had never conquered (and evangelized only, as it were, by accident in the person of Patrick, the imperfect Roman), fearlessly brought the ancient civilization back to its ancient home."[177]

1859 (give or take a couple of years)

The reach of Irish Christianity was at its zenith between the 500s-700sAD, after which it began to contract. Viking raiders arrived for the first time in 793AD, the first of many appearances over the coming decades in which they burned and ransacked monasteries, killing monks and raping nuns in the process.[178] Naturally Irish missionary endeavour took a major hit when monasteries could no longer train and send with their former efficiency. Then in the twelfth century the Vatican began to stamp its authority on the Irish church, which had been essentially a renegade free-church until that time, and the English invaded at the request of the pope to enforce this reformation.[179] (The Irish have largely forgiven the papacy for this, but not the English.) To do total injustice to the events between the height of monastic missionaries and the 1800s, basically an entire millennium, Christianity in Ireland became diluted, formalised, politicised and divided.[180] That's not to say there was nothing good, but it was a far cry from being

---

[177] Cahill, *How The Irish Saved Civilization*, pages 187-188
[178] Crawford Gribben, *The Rise And Fall Of Christian Ireland*, page 62-64
[179] Crawford Gribben, *The Rise And Fall Of Christian Ireland,*, 69-76
[180] Ibid, page, 57-121

the leading nation of Christian devotion and education on the planet

Now I am by no means about to declare that the outpouring of 1859 in Ulster was a full return to former glory; we're not exactly the land of saints and scholars once again. I do believe, however, that it was a glimpse of something, namely the past and the future of Christianity in our land, and furthermore its impact on present day Northern Irish Christianity is still being felt. Historian J Edwin Orr would agree with me, claiming in his study that the Ulster Revival had the greatest spiritual impact on Ireland than any event since Patrick.[181]

Before getting into the events of the revival proper, it's worth mentioning one essential ingredient in the build-up to it. Presbyterianism, the denomination where the revival originated, was plagued by Arian heresy in the early 1800s.[182] Originating with Arius in the third century, this teaching essentially stated that Jesus was not fully God, but a messenger from God, a sort of super angel, and was condemned by the church at the Council of Nicea in 325AD.[183] (Interestingly St Nicholas - yes, that St Nicholas, the Christmas one - actually stood so firmly against Arianism that he hit Arius in the face at that council. Two lessons here: early church leadership conferences were wild, and Santa punches heretics.)[184] The Arian false teaching has become prominent on multiple occasions since then, and the Presbyterian Church of Ireland almost embraced it. Fortunately a

---

[181] J Edwin Orr, *The Second Evangelical Awakening In Britain* (Marshall, Morgan and Scott Ltd, 1949) page 57
[182] Crawford Gribben, *The Rise And Fall Of Christian Ireland,*, 149
[183] https://www.britannica.com/topic/Arianism accessed 14th December 2021
[184] https://www.stnicholascenter.org/who-is-st-nicholas/stories-legends/traditional-stories/life-of-nicholas/bishop-nicholas-loses-his-cool accessed 14th December 2021

minister named Henry Cooke, after years of argument, division and courageous leadership, managed to expel the Arians from the denomination and affirm the doctrine of the Trinity, ensuring that the entire denomination held to conservative Protestant orthodoxy.[185] Without this yeoman's work in the 1830s, it's unlikely that the 1859 Ulster revival would have happened. In my first chapter I said that God often moves differently at different times, and in this instance a theological dogfight in one generation led to an outpouring of the Spirit in the next.

But nonetheless, the Ulster revival came at a low ebb in Northern Irish Protestantism. The famine of the 1840s had decimated the population through starvation and emigration, and those left were under a cloud of despondency, turning to whiskey as only the depressed Irish can.[186] Meanwhile the church was *"altogether Laodicean"* according to one minister - meaning lukewarm - and another described his congregation as *"dead to God, formal, cold, prayerless, worldly and stingy in religious things,"* before saying, *"What alarmed me most was the indisposition, almost hostility of the people to meet for prayer."* A third claimed, *"I had preached the gospel faithfully, earnestly, and plainly for eleven years; yet it was not known to me that a single individual had been converted."*[187]

Then in Ballymena, a young man named James McQuilken was saved whilst listening to the conversation of an English missionary called Mrs

---

[185] Crawford Gribben, *The Rise And Fall Of Christian Ireland,*, 149-151
[186] Pettie, *Do It Again Lord*, page 52
[187] First read in Pettie's *Do It Again Lord*, page 53 but was not footnoted
Original quotes from William Reid, *Authentic Records of Revival, now in progress in the United Kingdom* (J. Nisbet & Company, 1860) page 216-217

Colville.[188] Returning to his home village of Kells a few miles away, his friends saw a change in him and three of them were saved through his witness in the following months. In September of 1857, the four of them made a covenant to meet each week for prayer and Bible study, with no particular designs on anything other than growing in their faith.[189] It wasn't until New Year's Day, 1858, that they saw their first prayer answer: the conversion of a farm servant friend. Another was converted shortly thereafter and added to the prayer meeting. Stirred by their early success and encouraged by reports of a move of God in America, McQuilken decided to pray for a revival. He got it.

The prayer meeting grew, and then multiplied, and those prayer meetings also grew and multiplied, until there were a hundred prayer meetings taking place in and around the village every week.[190] The revival was contagious. Around Kells, Connor and Ballymena, people began to be saved in droves. Thousands gathered out in the rain, heard God's word, and 'fell on their knees in the mud of the streets'.[191] Orr says, "*Drunkards, blasphemers, harlots, thieves, on the one hand, and the respectable, the moral, the educated and the intelligent on the other, were instantaneously converted to a new way of life.*"[192]

Struck by conviction, people began to fall flat on the ground under the power of God. One '*wicked lad*', eighteen years of age, decided it would be a good idea to stand at the door of churches, scoffing and swearing at the converts. When the minister denounced him as a scorner, he "*was struck to the ground as by lightning, and,*

---

[188] Orr, *The Second Evangelical Awakening In Britain* page 38
[189] Pettie, *Do It Again Lord*, page 57-58
[190] Ibid, page 63
[191] Orr, 40
[192] Orr, 40

after lying as one dead, awakened to pray: "Lord, save me; I perish!"' and went around telling people never to mock the move of God.[193] Stories like this were commonplace; some were awakened by angels warning them of their death if they did not repent, others stayed up all night under conviction, others could not stop singing for joy, whilst other whole groups of twenty to thirty were prostrated under the power of God before being saved.

Then revival swept from the Presbyterians to all evangelicals, and from Kells and Ballymena to Belfast and all of Ulster.[194] It rocked the nation, seemingly overnight. Such large crowds attended churches that they had to be dismissed, with worries that the balconies would cave in under the weight.[195] One minister wrote, *"The difficulty used to be to get the people into the Church, but the difficulty now is to get them out."*[196] Regular open air services were conducted across the province to accommodate the crowds, tens of thousands turning up without the desperate marketing of today's revivalistic attempts. Sinners were reborn with wet eyes, bent knees, and transformed hearts. New songs were written. Crime dramatically decreased. In County Antrim, for a period there were no prisoners in custody and no crimes reported at all. Drunkenness fell through the floor, shutting pubs across the province. Sectarian marches were turned into times of prayer.[197]

By the end of this period, no more than a couple of years in length, conservative estimates reckon that one

---

[193] Orr, 41
[194] Pettie, Do It Again Lord, 63-74
Orr, 44-57
[195] Orr, 39-40
[196] Samuel Prime, *Five Years of Prayer, with the Answers* (Harper, 1864) page 270
[197] Pettie, Do It Again Lord, 63-74
Orr, 44-57

hundred thousand people had been converted.[198] One hundred thousand people, in a province with just over 1.4 million inhabitants at the time.[199] In two years.

Within Ulster, that revival has paved the way for the strong evangelical presence that remains to this day. From the Elim movement of the early 1900s, to the work of W.P. Nicholson in the 1920s, to the Free Presbyterian movement of the 1960s, to the Charismatic movement in the 1990s - regardless of your personal perspective on any of them - they all owe a great deal of debt to the mighty move of God in 1859.

As before in our history, the revival on this island spread to the one to our east. A similar move of God broke out in Scotland, with the Scottish saints inspired to pray based on happenings in Ulster.[200] The Welsh likewise had an outpouring, also with a hundred thousand converts, and no, that's not the same one as in 1905.[201] England was next, and the move of God there led not only to hundreds of thousands of salvations in each region of the nation, but to the establishment and the dramatic growth of Dr Barnardo's Homes, the Sunday-school movement, Christian Unions, the YMCA, the Evangelical Alliance, the Keswick Convention and the Salvation Army. This impact on Britain led to subsequent revivals in the West Indies and India, pioneering missions in Africa, and Hudson Taylor's influence in China.[202]

Whilst we don't get to pat ourselves on the back for what people experienced in the past, and even at the time Ulster certainly couldn't lay claim to all of the

---

[198] Orr, 57
[199] https://en.wikipedia.org/wiki/Demography_of_Northern_Ireland accessed 14th December 2021
[200] Orr, 58-77
[201] Orr, 79
[202] Orr, 95-171, 208-229

above institutions by virtue of being slightly upstream from them, it does seem that being a catalyst for revival across these islands and an influence from here to the wider world is part of our spiritual heritage. Such an idea is perfectly in keeping with how God used Patrick and the early Irish missionary monks. We were rocked by a glorious move of the Spirit, saved from darkness and despair, before that movement and that salvation leapt from here to Britain, and then onto distant shores. When God has desired to change the world in ages past, He has sometimes started here. My prayer is that we remember this heritage and that we might believe for Him to do so once again. Goodness me, don't we need it?

Discussion Questions

1 – What is your favourite story of revival on our island, and why?

2 – What impact have those previous revivals had on your church, your faith or our province, that perhaps you have never known or noticed before?

3 – Do you believe that Northern Ireland has a calling from God to reach the Western world, and if so, what does that look like today? If not, what do you believe Northern Ireland is called to be and do?

4 – What challenged you about these stories, and what will you do differently having been challenged in that way?

CHAPTER 5
THAT'LL LEARN YE
Or: A Strategy For Revival In Our Day

I'd like to begin this by acknowledging that my subtitle for this chapter is stupid. You can't strategise a revival any more than you can strategise an earthquake. Attempts to artificially create one, say by planting explosives in the ground and setting them off, might lead to a little tremor, but if we think that's the same as a 9.0 on the Richter-scale city-flattener, we're seriously underestimating what 'The Big One' looks like. Quite frankly, setting up a man-made revival and thinking 'that'll do' is an act of profound unbelief. We need a God-ordained one.

But like an earthquake, though a God-ordained revival isn't something you can manufacture, it is something you can prepare for. The Spirit may be like the wind, blowing where He pleases, but that doesn't mean you can't stick up a sail and go along for the ride. In fact to do so is a necessary component of revival.

Selwyn Hughes, Welsh minister and author of multiple books on spiritual awakenings, writes that in revival, as in all things, the sovereignty of God and the responsibility of man go hand in hand. In his daily devotional, he likens them to train tracks, saying, *"these two thoughts (are) like two rails that run from one end of the Scriptures to the other... If you try to keep to only one rail you finish up being derailed.*"[203] I agree with his idea of considering both, but I would go further. Two parallel rails, by definition, never meet. Divine sovereignty and human responsibility, on the other hand, can never separate.

Though a revival cannot be manufactured by human endeavour, when God sends one it always starts in the activity of the church. You could say that a longing for and expectation of revival is actually the beginning of a revival, and though that beginning does not necessarily look like the rushing floodwater of God's power and presence, it is the first crack in the dam after which it's simply a matter of time before the deluge. Once the church is stirred to seek God with urgency and persistence, refusing to stop until they see Him move, revival is ultimately inevitable. It might not look like they planned, or come on their timeline, or line up with their every wish, but it will come.

Think about the Wesleyan revival in the 1700s. John Wesley began preaching in the open country in around 1739, after not merely months, but years of failed ministry. In 1735 he had travelled to the colony of Georgia as a missionary, before returning in disgrace a couple of years later.[204] His preaching in England upon his return was received about as badly as possible; church leaders kept asking him not to come back, his style being too common and his message too abrasive for their liking.[205] His own spiritual walk was plagued by doubt and fear.[206] Then in 1739, because no church

---

[203] Selwyn Hughes, *Every Day Light* (B&H Publishing Group, 1997) page 356
[204] https://www.britannica.com/biography/John-Wesley accessed 15th December 2021
[205] https://christianhistoryinstitute.org/magazine/article/john-wesley-and-18th-century-timeline accessed 15th December 2021
[206] https://www.methodist.org.uk/about-us/the-methodist-church/history/a-storm-at-sea/ accessed 15th December 2021

would have him, he started preaching in fields, and tens of thousands showed up to hear him with mass conversions among the lower rungs of society following.[207] This was the beginning of the greatest revival in English history, one which travelled across the Atlantic, changing Britain and America for centuries to come.[208]

Or was it? Not: 'was it a great revival?' but rather: 'was that the beginning?' I think it started much earlier. In 1729, together with his friend George Whitefield and his brother Charles, Wesley helped to found and lead the Holy Club at Oxford University. This group of men gathered for prayer, Bible study and good works, and a determination to impact the world around them. Together they developed a rule of life that was strict, prayerful and devout.[209] Now, I'll confess, it might be that these men were not even truly saved at this point; both Wesley and Whitefield attest to later events in the mid-1730s that were vital moments of awakening, and potentially even rebirth.[210] However, I do not doubt that God used their spiritual determination not only to save them, if indeed they needed salvation at that point, but as the catalyst for the future awakenings. They sought God with all their hearts, and as Jeremiah promises, they found Him. The revival started in the Holy Club a decade before the crowds gathered in fields, not as a full-grown oak tree but as an acorn. Once these men

---

[207] https://hackingchristianity.net/2018/10/wesley-didnt-say-it-persistence-and-preaching.html - accessed 15th December 2021
[208] For further reading, 'George Whitefield 'by Arnold Dallimore (Banner of Truth, 1970) and 'The Burning Heart, John Wesley' by A. Wood (Emeth Press, 2007)
[209] https://www.wesleysoxford.org.uk/people/holy-club/what-was-the-holy-club accessed 15th December 2021
[210] https://banneroftruth.org/uk/resources/articles/2005/george-whitefield-revival-preacher/ accessed 15th December 2021
https://www.methodist.org.uk/media/4339/2850_aldersgate_feast_of_faith_material_-_why_aldersgate.pdf accessed 15th December 2021

determined by to pursue God as they did, a revival of some sort was guaranteed.

Revival cannot happen simply by our effort, but neither can it happen without it. In all of this, God is the primary mover; He places a hunger in our hearts to seek a move, and then takes it upon Himself to satisfy us. It's not that the church has somehow forced God's hand; it's that His hand has moved them to prepare the way for the fullness of what He wants to do. A sure sign that God wants to send a revival is that we want Him to. The next step is that we must do something.

So what do we need to do? Well we've just done a whirlwind tour of the rich spiritual history of Ireland in general and Ulster in particular. Some might think that the worst thing we could do would be to forget it. I agree, this would be the worst thing. However the second worst thing would be to remember it and learn nothing. That would be like building a majestic edifice to commemorate past triumphs in battle, then going inside it to burn all our weapons. And after that, giving Germany a call to see if they still have anyone called Adolf still knocking around, because if so, would he fancy another crack? Such remembrance serves only to leave us with the miserable knowledge that victory is both glorious and possible but not something we will ever experience. To use another common analogy, there's no point standing on the shoulders of giants if at some point you don't open your eyes to see something from the improved vantage point. Success is not just to be remembered, it is to be built on and repeated.

Recognising that some readers won't necessarily take the time to think through all the lessons to be learned from our past revivals on their own - not you of course, you're brilliant, but the others - it seems like it'd be remiss of me not to point them out. You'll find that they're not much more than the basic lessons of Scripture on this topic. Entire books have been written on each item here, so it won't be possible to cover them fully when bunching them all together in a single chapter. But there's some practical application for our specific context here that other more general works might not give. And part of the Christian walk is not simply to have once known what we ought to do, but to remind ourselves of it and be stirred up to actually do it today.

Pray

Part of me is tempted to just write 'Duh' in this section and say no more, but I'm not sure it would be edifying, even if it is appropriate. Because realistically we all know that every single move of God in history has not happened without prayer. Serious prayer. Continuous prayer. Urgent prayer. Prayer and fasting. Yet for some reason we struggle to do it. Why is this?

Well, I think I have an answer. Get this, it's genius: we struggle to pray because prayer is difficult. I know, I know, I can practically hear the standing ovations across the world as people read this. Notify the Nobel Prize committee for this astonishing breakthrough ASAP. I could use the money.

Here's the thing though: the reason why we struggle to pray when it's difficult is that we've likely all had times in the past when prayer was easy. I sincerely hope so anyway. As believers, often early in our walk, or in certain seasons of life, we should have times of prayer where it seems like the presence of God is so close we could reach out and touch Him. We should have seasons where hours seem like minutes at the throne of God. There should be times when there is a simple, joyful flow in prayer that you never want to stop.

Our problem is that once we have experienced that, that is all we ever want prayer to be, and we don't imagine it can or should be anything different. We tend to think that if we go into the place of prayer and it doesn't look like that, but is instead dry and slow, that either we are praying wrong, or worse, that God doesn't want us to pray.

This is a particular problem in our day and age, when everything is based around emotional satisfaction and little else. Rather than considering that God might want to build something in us of perseverance, of spiritual diligence, or of simply getting us beyond the fleeting emotions that drive our lives, we instead prefer to find something else to do with our time when prayer doesn't do the trick. Facebook and Netflix can give us the easy dopamine hit we're not currently receiving from God.

That's not to say that we could not indeed be praying wrong, or that God could never call us to do anything other than prayer. Of course we might be praying wrong: our focus might be too much on ourselves, or we might need to pray with others, or we might need to come in repentance first, to suggest some options. And God, though calling us to live lives of constant prayer, doesn't call us to live lives of only prayer. There's work to be done, children to raise, spouses to be loved and a world to be reached, all to the glory of God.

It is to say, however, that everything worthwhile is an equal mix of glory and grit. Work, childrearing, marriage and evangelism are not a lazy river ride on a suitably-inflated lilo with a pina colada in your hand. They all have moments of extraordinary happiness alongside seasons of mundane repetition and plenty of hard grind. We may live in a world where people give up on such responsibilities the moment the feelings subside, hence our sky-high divorce rates, our absentee parenting styles and our inability to work a bog-standard job for more than twenty minutes, but that is not how believers should live. The fact that we don't 'feel it' doesn't exempt us from doing our duty before God in any of those areas, and neither does it exempt us when it comes to prayer. When you stand before God, He will not ask you how you felt when doing what He commanded you to do, He will simply ask you whether or not you did it. 'Did you pray without ceasing? No? No further questions.'

Now as I type this, I can hear a repeated metallic grinding noise in the background as people sharpen their knives, all emblazoned with the word 'legalism' on the side. There's an echo of ten thousand upon ten thousand voices, chanting the words in Matthew 6, *"Do not heap up empty phrases like the Gentiles, who think they will be heard for their many words."*[211]

So before I get lynched in the name of God's boundless grace, let me explain that what Jesus was attacking here was the prayer techniques of unbelievers who thought that their gods could be appeased and coerced with mindless chanting. He was opposed to using prayer as a way to right-standing with God, assuming He could be manipulated into submission or impressed with our efforts. Instead of using prayer as a bargaining chip with

---

[211] Matthew 6:7

God, He instead instructed us to observe the joyful, free access we have to the Father, and use it regularly. The total time in prayer for superstitious unbelievers and believers might be the same, nay, it should be greater for us, but the motivation is the exact opposite. The danger is dead religion and works righteousness, not continuing to pray when the warm fuzzies don't hit just right.

To really hammer home my point, this same Jesus is the one who told an entire parable to encourage us *"that we ought always to pray and not lose heart,"* and that His elect should *"cry to him day and night."*[212] By definition, then, there might be times when we pray and *could* lose heart. There *are* times when it *might not* feel great. But we should pray regardless. Lots. Discipline is not legalism.

For the life of me I couldn't track down the following story, but trust me that I read it somewhere. Or at least that I remember reading it somewhere, and that it is my memory rather than my honesty that's at stake here. Anyway, a senior church leader was sitting with some small-group leaders, discussing prayer topics. One of them raised that he felt bad for not praying more for his group members. The others, in true post-modern style, leapt immediately to the small-group leader's defence, saying that he should not feel condemned and that he was trying his best. They were obviously sincere and well-meaning, however the senior leader felt there might be more to it than that. He said, "I think maybe God wants you to pray for your people more." Profound! The small-group leader agreed that this was

---

[212] Luke 18:1-9

probably right, and rather than feeling condemned, decided to pray more for his people.

Whilst this sounds like a simple story, most of us default to the attitude of the other leaders, who assume God is constantly satisfied with our prayer life merely because we wish it was better. We rarely think that He might want to stretch us in this area, and actually, you know, get better at it.

One of our key problems is not that we have so much over-spiritualised prayer, expecting too much from time set aside with God, as we have under-spiritualised routine. We have assumed that doing something over and over can have no spiritual benefit if we don't have goosebumps and sheer elation every time we do it. Imagine we took the same attitude with brushing our teeth, or talking to our wives, or jogging. God is the God of more than our feelings, and He doesn't tire of repetition. He makes the sun get up every morning, He makes the flowers bloom every spring, He runs the water cycle every moment of every day. And He hears our requests with gladness every time we ask, no matter how we feel about it. Yet we think it doesn't work without an emotional kick. Chapter and verse on that one, please.

Does it not strike anyone as interesting that all the great revivals of our past have been fuelled by committed, regular, persistent, and most often corporate prayer? Ok, St Patrick might have 'prayed a hundred times' a day and again at night - likely meaning saying the Lord's prayer - on his own, but even then he still ticks three out of four boxes. Do you really think that on day one thousand and forty-three, on his eighty-seventh repetition of the day, the words 'Our Father' made him tingle with delight? Or the monks - remember their centuries-long prayer meeting at Bangor and the strict hours of prayer? Do you reckon the guys on the 3 AM shift, in the middle of a fast, hitched up their habits and danced a merry jig out of bed in the morning? Or McQuilken and his buddies, praying in a barn in the dead of winter with no results each week - does that sound gratifying, or more like gruelling? I think part of the reason it was mostly corporate - aside from that being by far the most common biblical pattern for prayer - is that hard work needs accountability. It's too easy to skip it if you're on your own.

Then again, does any of us really think revival will come without some sort of cost to our comfort? We begin to pay it through sacrificial ongoing prayer. I have a word from God for almost everyone reading this book: pray more.

Have courage

I normally get a bit hot and bothered when I hear sermons about 'do not fear'. Not because the concept itself isn't wholly biblical and necessary to hear, but because of the way it is most often applied. Sermons on this subject tend to pair the Biblical exhortations to courage with vague applications to seemingly irrational fears, like a parent teaching a child not to be afraid of the dark because there really isn't anything scary lurking behind the wardrobe. Then, landing with graceful poise, the message closes with an exhortation to have a snuggle under the covers with Jesus because 'perfect love casts out all fear'.

Of course, irrational fear is a problem, but if you spend time reading the actual context of these commandments not to be afraid, they rarely if ever address some unjustifiable emotion, and rather speak about how we should act when faced with things that genuinely should terrify us. The apostle John, who wrote that nifty screensaver verse about perfect love casting out all fear, was not only exiled, but boiled in oil for his faith.[213] That's the biblical context for overcoming fear. Yet somehow I rarely see his verse, written with fine calligraphy, neatly placed atop an image of someone scarred for life for their gospel witness.

Historical revivals have never been poured out upon cowards. Indeed, rather than promising rich blessings of God's presence on spiritual saps, Revelation places cowards alongside idolaters and murderers in the fire of hell, because a coward will deny the faith once the temperature of persecution rises.[214] When God has wanted to use a coward for something great, say like the apostle Peter, the first thing He does is make them not a coward by filling them with the Spirit. Only then are they a suitable revival vessel. Revival demands that we take this commandment and put it to real work, stretching it to its limits with things that would cause a natural man to flee a mile in the other direction.

Think about the mission of St Patrick, returning the nation from which he had fled, with no support network, armed with only a Bible, and immediately defying the high king right out in the open. Think of the monks that came after, sailing around the world in leather boats only to face potential execution from

---

[213] https://www.britannica.com/biography/Saint-John-the-Apostle accessed 16th December 2021
[214] Revelation 20:8

Pictish and Frankish lords on arrival. Even think about our more recent ancestors in 1859, who faced constant ridicule from within the church and without for their 'fanaticism'. Do you think any of these guys had therapists to help them deal with their trauma? We can celebrate with hindsight the fact that God showed up to save many of their would-be persecutors, but they didn't know at the time that's how things would end. For all Patrick knew, he could have died on arrival, Columcille could have been beheaded by the Scottish, and Columbanus might have been burned at the stake for taking on the ecclesiastical hierarchy. Like them, we are not told that everything is going to work out before pursuing of a move of God; we're simply told, 'Don't be afraid' and sent out, knowing that Christ will ultimately succeed even if we do not.

So what kind of courage do we need? Unlike them we can successfully arrive at most places with relative safety, air travel and cars making sure getting to the mission field not a high-risk endeavour. And does this only apply to international missions? What about here in Northern Ireland, or in the Western world as a whole?

If you want an opportunity to demonstrate biblical courage, you're in luck. One of the key words in the book of Acts is 'bold' or 'boldness', appearing thirteen times in my translation. And each of these times, without exception, it is about talking to people about the gospel. However, by that I don't mean that we need the sort of courage that helps us quietly say, "Do you know Jesus loves you and has a wonderful plan for your life?" That is true, but that's not the fullness of the gospel, and it's not how the gospel was preached in the book of Acts.

Such preaching requires a minuscule amount of courage at most. No; if you read through the sermons of Acts, you will find that all of them, bar the one given to penitent Gentiles at the house of Cornelius, specifically address, by name, the sins of the people listening. In Jerusalem, the crowds were told that they crucified Jesus. In Athens, the crowds were told that they worshipped idols. The Pharisees were told that they were stiff-necked murderers. Jews in the diaspora were told that they were scoffers. The preaching of the gospel in Acts was directed at the specific sins of the group to whom it was being preached, urging them to repent of those sins, and then receive by faith the marvellous forgiveness available in Jesus. It was not some vague spiritual principle about a generic loving being who only wants to make you happy. It was: you are committing this sin, you need to turn away from it and be forgiven, and the good news is: you can be. That kind of preaching takes courage. It's the sort of preaching that causes either a revival or a riot, and nothing in between.

It's also the difference between fully preaching the gospel and not preaching it at all. We often talk about the death, burial and resurrection of Jesus, as they did, and which is the heart of the gospel. But when we refuse to mention any actual sins that need forgiven, or we explicitly avoid mentioning the sins that our hearers actually commit and talk only about the sins other people commit, we have failed to apply the gospel to them. We are demonstrating that a remedy exists for something, but not suggesting that anyone nearby actually needs it, and being very clear that we will by no means be the ones to administer it. This is not how any biblical preacher - from Moses to the prophets, and from Jesus to the apostles - preached. Such preaching is like stacking a bunch of TNT in the corner, running a wire to it, and then refusing to light the fuse. Nothing goes boom.

How does that play out in our day? Well, just try standing up and confronting the people of our age about their wild obsession with sexual immorality, from fornication to homosexuality. Or confront the denial of the basic truth that in the beginning, God made them male and female, no matter what you feel inside. Or confront them on the commandment: do not murder - even if it's an unborn child. Or say that theft and covetousness are sins, even if it's achieved by a vote to take more of your wealthy neighbour's stuff. Or talk about dishonouring your parents, which includes despising their faith, culture and way of life, and calling them bigots. Tell them that Jesus loves them and wants to forgive them *for those sins*. As I said, we have plenty of opportunity to demonstrate biblical courage. We just don't want to.

That kind of preaching will produce a reaction. A flammable age will accuse you of being inflammatory, and a hyper-politicised generation will say you are too political. And believers will say you're a Christian nationalist as you call your nation to repent.[215]

When this happens, don't worry, they did the same thing to the early church. Early Christians weren't persecuted by the Romans because the Romans disagreed with any claims about how nice Jesus was. Lol. Romans were comparatively religiously free, didn't require anyone to convert to their religion, and were

---

[215] Ripped this almost directly from Doug Wilson - see the relevant video here - https://www.youtube.com/watch?v=zQgfbhTRl3I accessed 16th December 2021
and also the 'Christian nationalist issue here - https://dougwils.com/books-and-culture/s7-engaging-the-culture/the-hard-bigotry-of-low-expectations.html accessed 16th December 2021

proud of their tolerance. You could keep your god, whatever it was, so long as you promised allegiance to Rome. And to do so, you had a simple task: take a pinch of incense, throw it on the fire that burned in front of the statue of Caesar, and say the words, *"Kaiser kurios"* - *"Caesar is lord."* Just once, and after that, worship your Jesus all you want, talk to people about Him, have church meetings, go nuts. But offer the incense, please. The early Christians flatly refused; they would not budge one inch, or rather, one pinch. And even though they were good, law-abiding, hard-working citizens, their persecution was because their gospel, which said that Jesus was Lord of all, put them in the category of 'political dissidents'.[216] Don't be surprised when they say the same sort of thing about you. Laugh, dodge the rocks, and keep preaching.

Is the aim to be incendiary? Not at all; the aim is to be faithful. But the two often look alike. So here's a simple rule for us Christians: preach the whole Bible. Do so fully aware of where it challenges the spirit of our age, and at those crossroads make sure not to pull any punches. You don't have to go out of your way to find trouble, just stick close to God's word and trouble will find you. At which point, have courage.

I need to add that training in cowardice is no way to prepare for the time when everything is on the line and you must either have courage or deny the faith. Don't think that years of silence, compromise and denial in small challenges is setting you up for anything other than silence, compromise and denial when in big ones. You must practise courage in small things. I'm attempting to raise my three-year-old son to be the kind

---

[216] R C Sproul, *Following Christ* (Tyndale House, 1991) page 35

of man who would jump in front of a bus to save a baby if needs be. We're working on it now by getting him to jump off the sofa into my arms. He is encouraged, coaxed and rewarded for bravery, and taught that even if the worst happens, it's not all that bad. He'll graduate from sofas, to bunk beds, to trees, to seaside cliffs. Courage does not strike from on high like a lightning bolt; it grows like wheat, from root, to shoot, to stalk, to ear.

If you lack courage, grow some. Find your own sofa, and leap off regularly. When they ask you to wear a rainbow badge every June, say no. When they ask why, say why. "I don't agree with it." Listen to bold preachers, and actually share their stuff. Recommend this book to someone. When abortion, transgenderism, or sexual immorality come up in conversation, don't be overbearing, but don't be silent. Say something. Take the flack with a smile, and offer to pray for everyone at the end. Lose your job and get another one. The direction of your life will be less defined by one big act of courage and more by a thousand little ones. Even if the worst happens and you die for your faith, it's not that bad; they can't touch your soul. Get courage. We won't have revival without it.

Get power, always pioneer, expect partisanship

Alright, so I have to bunch a few topics together here, because I have one last big topic to hit at the end of this chapter, and I'm going to run out of space if I don't. However I don't feel like I'd do justice to these lessons from previous revivals if I didn't at least give them a fleeting mention.

Firstly, we desperately need the power of God. Look, the above concept of courage perfectly coincides with being the worst marketing strategy in history. Good marketing is inoffensive, with broad appeal, ruling no one out from access to whatever it is you are selling. Biblically faithful courage is wildly offensive, a stumbling block to the Jews and foolishness to the Greeks; it has no appeal to anyone, being the stench of death to unbelievers; and rules literally everyone out from the kingdom by works except for Jesus, who willingly receives all who come to Him by grace. If we are going to have any chance of success, we need God to show up. The only thing that could convince our lost and dying world to even give us a hearing is the demonstration that what we are saying, however outrageous it may sound, is true.

I write as a convinced continuationist, meaning that I believe all the spiritual gifts outlined in Scripture are still available to the church today, including tongues, prophecy, healing and miracles. In my head there's no problem with monks in Ireland working wonders, or the dramatic, physical manifestations of God's presence that accompanied the revival in 1859. But this isn't a book on that topic, and I don't have space to make a full case here.

Instead, what I'll say is this: whether you are a charismatic or a cessationist, if you are a Christian of any sort then you believe in the power of God. We might disagree on some things, particularly on the semantics of what a gift of the Spirit is, but we all believe that God is at work in the world today, transforming hearts, doing miracles, and leading His people. We might disagree as to whether some healing miracle qualifies as a gift of miracles or simply a miraculous answer to prayer, but

I've heard enough cessationists preach to know that they believe God can heal the sick today. We might disagree on whether God's leading is the 'voice of the Spirit' or simply Him stirring our heart, but we all believe God can direct our paths. Either way, we all agree that God is present and active in His world today.

If we are to have a revival, we do not need to have a fully agreed upon theology of all these things, but we do have to have a wholehearted expectation and hunger for them. We're told to lay hands on the sick; let's do it. We're told to ask for God to lead us; let's ask. We're told that he can save even the worst of sinners; let's intercede until He does. Heaven must be let loose on the earth, transforming hearts, minds, bodies, individuals and nations to the glory of God. If heaven does not invade earth then hell most certainly will, and we'll be finished before we start.

The second and third areas of this little subsection go hand in hand, with pioneering and partisanship rarely found apart from each other in the context of revival.

Revivals, without fail, lead to the church reaching new groups of people, whether it be unreached nations, new tribes within nations, or simply bringing genuine life to nominal Christians who have not yet been transformed by the presence of God. Consider Saint Patrick, the Irish monks, and the 1859 revival respectively.

As this original pioneering work happens, combined with the mass transformation of society, what usually accompanies it is that, whilst many new bonds are formed among those impacted by the move of God, the existing religious leadership opposes it. Rather than recognising the move of God as something to be embraced and learning the lessons it could bring to them, they see it as a threat, reject it and try to kill it.

Under Saint Patrick, for instance, the druid leadership were either converted or wholeheartedly against the preaching of the gospel. Columbanus' ministry in Europe, even as it reached remote tribes, functioned as a rebuke to the luxurious lifestyles, evangelistic laxity and compromised teaching of the established churches. In 1859, though hundreds of thousands of evangelical believers of other stripes welcomed what God was doing, several of the leading Presbyterian ministers of the day rejected the awakening that began in their own denomination.[217]

Such a reaction is no departure from what we see in Scripture. Jesus brought together a gang that included zealots and tax collectors - natural political enemies - and wealthy upper-class accountants alongside blue-collar fishermen. There was a fresh, surprising unity. But there was also major division; the Pharisees and Sadducees sought to discredit Him, excommunicate Him and even put Him to death from an early point. In Acts, Jew and Gentile were united by one gospel and one Spirit, but the unbelieving Jewish leadership were the primary instigators of persecution against the people of God. This does not mean that the believers were at fault; the Jesus who prays that we should be one in John 17 also says that He came to bring division in Luke 12.

The reason for this persecution - as implied multiple times in the gospels, and stated explicitly and repeatedly in Acts - was crude jealousy. They didn't like that someone else could come along and draw such a crowd. Often the next move of God is most fiercely persecuted

---

[217] Pettie, *Do It Again Lord*, page 74-75

by the last one, because they are the group that senses the loss most keenly. Interestingly, they are the also the ones who then make the accusation that those involved in the new move of God are divisive.

This cycle of pioneering followed by rejection inevitably leads to further pioneering. The people transformed by the move of God need congregations that will receive them, so new churches are planted. They are barred from the normal means of public communication, so they find new ways to do so, whether they gather in monasteries, fields, or barns to spread their message. Old wineskins are chucked out, and new ones put to work.

And what are we to think about all this? Well, Christians tend to moan when new churches are planted, arguing that it detracts from existing congregations in the area. But the simple fact is that every revival in history has produced new churches by necessity. There has been no space for that move of God in the existing church; it's too offensive, too radical, and the new leaders are usually accused of being too arrogant to fit within the existing boundaries. This even happened to Jesus, who was received in Nazareth with cries of: "Who on earth does this guy think He is?" Many churches do the same with the prophetic voices of their own day, pushing out what God is currently doing because it might damage the nice museum they've built in honour of what He once did long ago. (That's not an excuse for actual arrogance, but confidently saying 'thus says the Lord' about things God actually says doesn't fit the bill.)

It's not that all old churches lack life, or that all new ones have it, but rather that old churches which are full of life will not be threatened by new ones. They will celebrate new churches, because Jesus says that the harvest is plentiful and it is the workers who are few. Any church's aim, old or new, should not be to acquire a bigger slice of the same fixed pie of pre-existing believers in an area but rather to see more people saved. More workers means more harvest.

Churches that fail to recognise this will eventually go out of business. Most believers reel in horror at such a notion, but the fact is that some churches absolutely have to die. Jesus Himself killed several, and if you don't believe me, read what happened to the congregations named in Revelation 1-3. Ultimately if Christ's return is not for another thousand years, it's very likely that every church currently in existence will go extinct before that time, and subsequently be replaced by new, life-filled churches. That is absolutely fine. Though it's not wrong to try and turn a church around - it's noble, and often the best place to start - if it is not received, then shake off the dust and move on pronto. God's move will not wait.

We must not love the institution more than the mission. Our temptation is to think that the death of a local church organisation is a sad and terrible thing; but if that church has long-since abandoned its original purpose then its death is a comparative mercy. If my own church ever loses sight of its vision, I pray that it goes down in flames immediately, to be replaced by a new one that honours our original DNA.

In conclusion, if God is moving and your church opposes it, do what you can. Firstly, ensure that it definitely is God, and listen carefully if someone disagrees and backs it up from Scripture. But if it is Him, politely and thoughtfully spend whatever relationship capital you have to try and get the leadership on board. Make sure that whatever way it goes, they will know that a prophet has been among them. Should you find some openness, however flawed it may be, then stay, fight and build. But if you have done all you reasonably can and they still reject it, leave. Leaving in that scenario is an act of loyalty to what the church purports to be.

Repent

So some of my favourite stories come from the Hebridean revival of 1949-1953. I'll admit, it's not technically Irish, however we did say that Columcille went to Iona, one of the Hebrides, like 1400 years before it happened. Does that count?

No. Probably not. But anyway, it illustrates my point well, so I'm going to use it.

Duncan Campbell, the key minister involved in this revival, gives the following example of the presence and power of God at work on the islands in that time.

> *"Over 100 young people were at the dance in the parish hall and they weren't thinking of God or eternity. God was not in all of their thoughts. They were there to have a good night when suddenly the power of God fell upon the dance. The music ceased and in a matter of minutes, the hall was empty. They fled from the hall as a man fleeing from a plague. And they made for the church. They are now standing outside. Oh, yes--they saw lights in the church. That was a house of God and they were going to it and they went. Men and women who had gone to bed rose, dressed, and made for the church. Nothing in the way of publicity--no mention of a special effort except and intonation from*

the pulpit on Sabbath that a certain man was going to be conducting a series of meetings in the parish covering 10 days. But God took the situation in hand--oh, He became His own publicity agent. A hunger and a thirst gripped the people."[218]

It is this kind of manifestation of God's presence that we are most in need of today. In a dark and disinterested generation, no mere amount of words or effort can do what only God can. Our main issue in the church is not a lack of people in our meetings, but a lack of presence. At some point, He must show up.

The question we should ask ourselves is: how do we get the presence of God in this way? Well, allow me to use the origin of the Hebridean revival as arguably the perfect illustration.

Two elderly ladies, Christine and Peggy Smith, were burdened for the spiritual state of the islands, and in particular the young people among the population. Not a single young person in their parish of Barvas attended church. So they committed themselves to pray each Tuesday, from 10pm-4am, calling on God to fulfil His promise that, *"I will pour water on him that is thirsty and floods upon the dry ground."*

One night, one of them had a vision of the church packed to the brim with young people, and a strange minister standing in the pulpit. They sent for the parish minister, and told him to gather his elders and spend Tuesday and Friday nights, from 10pm until the wee hours of the morning, in prayer. Perhaps remarkably, the elders agreed.

---

[218] https://www.revival-library.org/revival_histories/evangelical/twentieth_century/hebrides_revival_2.shtml accessed 20th December 2021

But six weeks in, and nothing had happened. Nothing at all, until one young man stood up, and according to Campbell, the following occurred:

> "... a deacon in the church, got up and read Psalm 24. "Who shall ascend the hill of God? Who shall stand in His holy place? He that has clean hands and a pure heart who has not lifted up his soul unto vanity or sworn deceitfully. He shall receive the blessing (not a blessing, but the blessing) of the Lord." And then that young man closed his Bible. And looking down at the minister and the other office bearers, he said this-maybe crude words, but perhaps not so crude in our Gaelic language-he said, "It seems to me to be so much humbug to be praying as we are praying, to be waiting as we are waiting, if we ourselves are not rightly related to God." And then he lifted his two hands-and I'm telling you just as the minister told me it happened-he lifted his two hands and prayed, "God, are my hands clean? Is my heart pure? " But he got no further. That young man fell to his knees and then fell into a trance. Now don't ask me to explain this because I can't. He fell into a trance and is now lying on the floor of the barn. And in the words of the minister, at that moment, he and his other office bearers were gripped by the conviction that a God-sent revival must ever be related to holiness, must ever be related to Godliness."[219]

That presence of God fell not only in the barn, but across the whole community that very night. It started a revival that lasted almost four years, with thousands of young

---

[219] https://www.revival-library.org/revival_histories/evangelical/twentieth_century/hebrides_revival_2.shtml accessed 20th December 2021

people saved and dramatic stories of supernatural conviction among even the hardest of hearts.

It strikes me as interesting that God's priority in the build-up to this revival was to deal with the sin of the church. Though He clearly desired to send a revival that saved the lost in huge number, He seemingly refused to do so until the people of God got on their face to deal with their *own* sin. And it doesn't seem like these men who gathered to pray were leading double-lives or doing any sin of great note. But nonetheless, they didn't have even a hint of revival until they came before God in repentance for their sins.

Reverting to my original question, how do we get the presence of God? The answer: the same as the elders of Barvas discovered, and which Psalm 24 tells us, "*Who may ascend the hill of the Lord, and who can stand in His holy place? He who has clean hands and a pure heart.*"

Without saying everything that can be said on the subject, this text refers to the Levitical practice of washing their hands before entering the temple. Such a washing was not about making atonement for sin; the priesthood had to sacrifice for their sins like everyone else, and mere washing couldn't cleanse them. As Hebrews says, 'without the shedding of blood, there is no remission of sins.'[220] So what was the purpose of the washing? To maintain sensitivity about sin before God, to stop anyone coming before Him casually, and to recognise His holiness. Before going into God's presence, one had to set one's mind on having a clean life in His sight.

This is not merely an Old Testament commandment, in case anyone would be tempted to write it off as such.

---

[220] Hebrews 9:22

James 4:8 says the exact same thing to believers, clearly echoing this text, as he says, "*Draw near to God, and he will draw near to you. Cleanse your hands, you sinners, and purify your hearts, you double-minded.*" (If anyone is wondering, no, James didn't preach the prosperity gospel.) Like the Old Testament priests, our cleanliness doesn't atone for sins, only the one true sacrifice does that, which has been fulfilled in Christ. But even though that sacrifice has been offered once for all, that doesn't mean we should come before God in irreverence, refusing to acknowledge our sin, or defending ourselves for it. If we want God's presence, we must come with a holy life, and ask for cleansing in those areas that need made clean.

As was the case for Patrick who was referred to in his vision as a '*holy youth*', as was true for the monks who were known for their separation from the sins of the world, and as it was in 1859 who were not only saved from the eternal punishment of their sins, but from continuing to commit them in this life to the extent that it reordered Northern Irish society, so must this passion for holiness must be true for us if we want to see a revival. It is not enough to desire that 'the world' would repent in order to see a move of God, or to think that 'someone else' needs to sort themselves out. If we want to see a revival, we ourselves must repent. It's not a thing for those 'out there', but rather far more important that we do so 'in here'.

That includes you. I know it's rare for someone to be so blunt in today's world, and it's much more socially acceptable to say, "I should repent" or, "We should repent," than, "You should repent." Though what I say here does of course relate to me too, this point needs to hit home before I end the chapter, so I say it to you: part of the reason we don't have a revival is your incomplete repentance. Mine too. The whole Christian life is to be one of repentance, according to Luther's first thesis, and I'm sure we can agree that if we all lived perfectly repentant lives we would certainly have an awakening.[221] Therefore if you *would like* to have one, view your own repentance as an essential element.

What should you repent of? That's not something I can say specifically for you personally, it'll be different for each reader. But in the interests of mortifying some flesh, let me give some suggestions. Assume that the ones that annoy you most are the ones you most likely need forgiveness for:

Prayerlessness. Pride. Spiritual lukewarmth. Unbelief. Liberal theology. Lifeless biblical conservatism. Empty worship. Idolatry of sports, money, sex, popularity, social acceptability, social media, entertainment, or anything else. Not worshipping with your whole heart.

Failure to evangelise. Legalism. Using God's name in vain. Neglecting Scripture reading. Not gathering for church. Failure to provide for elderly parents, whether physically or emotionally. Assuming the elder generation has nothing to offer you. Exasperating your kids. Gossiping about your parents. Having an abortion. Voting for abortion, even if you are 'personally opposed' to it. Drunkenness. Smoking weed. Swearing. Watching porn. Watching the not-quite-but-almost porn which makes up the most popular shows and movies today. Fornication. Sleeping around. Mental adultery. Actual

---

[221] Luther, Martin, *Works of Martin Luther With Introductions and Notes (Volume I)* (Philadelphia A. J. Holman Company, 1915) Kindle Edition, Location 382

adultery. Neglecting your wife. Disrespecting your husband. Speaking or acting abusively towards your kids. Voting for the destruction of the family through same-sex marriage. Illegally streaming. Cheating on your taxes. Laziness. Workaholism. Advocating 'justice' but not being personally generous. Not giving to church. Voting to take more of your neighbour's stuff. Giving without joy. Lying. Even white lies. Lying to your kids to get them to do what you want. Going along with societal-wide lies, like that there is a gender spectrum, or that people can actually transition from one gender to the other. Pretending to be oppressed to gain social power. Coveting other people's stuff. Gossiping. Thinking or saying the people down the road are all sectarian bigots. Being a sectarian bigot in thought, word or deed. Telling people who have little that they are by definition privileged due to skin colour. Actual racism. And many more.

Don't leave this in the theoretical; why not get on your knees before moving to the next chapter, and repent of whichever of the above apply to you? If you're offended, add that to the list, and repent for that too.

Discussion Questions

1 – How should you pray more for revival, and what should that prayer focus on for you personally?

2 – Have you lacked courage at any point, or seen a lack of courage in your immediate surroundings when it comes to clearly preaching the gospel to our world?

3 – How will you go about pursuing the power of God in your life?

4 – What does the need for pioneering mean for you personally, your church, and your denomination?

5 – What do you need to repent from?

CHAPTER 6
IT'LL
BE CLASS
Or: Why Revival Is Guaranteed

If I've judged things correctly thus far, I'm trusting that this book has caused an aura of gloom among my readership, as well as a good deal of outrage. Hearing about the state of the Northern Irish church as is, and the fact that we all need to get on our face before God to fix it because our sin is the primary issue at stake, should have that effect. So if that's where you're at, I've calculated it perfectly, albeit that my chances of either being published or widely read are now effectively zero. Sad times. But somehow you're here, so there's that.

However, alongside the sadness and anger, part of my aim has been to give a glimmer of hope along the way. Kind of like watching Northern Ireland play international football; it's mostly bad, but then David Healy gets in behind the English defence, smashes it home, and 'Away In A Manger' becomes impossible to sing without chanting about our greatest ever striker. "The stars in the bright sky looked down where Healy, Healy, Healy."

Where was I? Oh yes, the book.

I've not wanted to provide a false hope, some sort of chest-thumping, reality-denying, 'the church is really doing great' kind of hope, often found at certain big

Christian conferences but which only lasts until you walk out the door and see what's going on in the wider world. Our hope is not based on pretending something isn't happening when it is, but on the God who sits above it all, working all things together for the good of those who love Him. Our hope is not the kind that says Jesus was not really in the grave on the Saturday, but the kind that says He really walked out again on Sunday.

In this chapter, I want to double-down on that hope. I want this to be among the most hopeful chapters you ever read about the future of the world as a whole, and the future of our country in particular. My aim is to ensure you have a firm assurance that hope is the only reasonable way for a Christian to live. In spite of what we see right now, I am hopeful.

But before you assume I'm going to speak about the second coming and the reign of the saints in glory, no, I am not just talking about that kind of hope. That's amazing, of course,, but the promises of the kingdom go further than pie-in-the-sky-when-we-die, something good will happen after this world ends but not before. I am, of course, more hopeful about that eternity than anything else, but at the same time I am hopeful about more than that. I am also hopeful about the future of the church in Northern Ireland, and by extension the future of Northern Ireland, on this side of the return of Christ.

My position is this: when it comes to the future of the world before the return of Christ, I am a short-term realist but a long-term optimist. The short-term realism has two sides to it: firstly, I believe that unless we see a dramatic move of God, the church in the West is going to experience major decline, marginalisation, and potential persecution in the coming decades. Secondly, because I am still a Christian in my realism, I maintain the belief that God can intervene and change this even in our lifetime, rescuing us from short-term destruction by a powerful awakening, and that we should work to this end with confidence in His power to save. The long-term optimism looks as follows: I am absolutely convinced that such a revival is absolutely guaranteed in our future, and whether it comes in our generation or in one to come, Northern Ireland will be saved.

Some might be tempted to place the source of my hope with me and my generally sunny disposition, but I can assure you that's not the case. My confidence is in the promises of God, given to Christ and His church, concerning the future of the world. Importantly, it is based on what will happen prior to His return. I am wildly optimistic about the long term, because God's word is true and will be fulfilled, and it paints a picture of a brighter future than most of us would dare to imagine.

Now I'm aware that this view will run into some resistance. Most believers today have a dark picture of the future, with things getting worse and worse, major apostasy among the people of God, and a one-world government headed by an antichrist who will persecute the church and set up a statue of himself in the temple. Because this isn't a book intending to give a full explanation of how the future will play out, as though that were possible, I'm not going to even attempt to address the multitude of questions that will inevitably crop up. Answering how one can have a positive view of the future of humanity in a church context where it is assumed that the Bible says we're all going to hell in a handbasket, and at a time in history when that seems to be playing out before our eyes, is something that must really be done with a full book to be worthwhile. I simply don't have space to do that, plus there are already many great books on the topic. But I'll suggest some in the bibliography if you want further reading. All I'll say is this: if these promises are true - which they definitely are - and if I've interpreted them rightly - which is much less guaranteed, but still I believe my arguments are convincing - then we can believe for great things ahead in our world. Including a revival in Northern Ireland.

What I'm asking you as the reader to do is simple: for the remainder of this chapter, don't immediately fire back with, "But what about (insert major question here)?" Of course, there is an important place for that commendable kind of Berean attitude, but it would be better to do so whilst reading a book that attempts to answer such questions. I'm not going to do that. Instead, I'm asking you to give this perspective the temporary benefit of the doubt, after which you can dispense with it if you like. Preferably go further and read one of my recommended books on the topic, or several. But a fair hearing on these handful of verses, in context, is all I would like for now. It's not a major ask; although this view of the future might be rarer today, it is not only well within the bounds of orthodoxy, but has actually been the most common view for most of church history.

Stealing an idea from Douglas Wilson, it might help to simply treat this perspective like a marvellous work of fiction. When reading or watching a fictional story of any sort, you gain vastly more from the tale by setting aside the obvious objections to it. Of course there aren't Jedi, X-Wings or lightsabers; of course there is no land called Narnia full of talking beavers; and Finn MacCool never built a Causeway. But if, whilst engaging in such a story, you stopped every few minutes to say, "Hey, this is nonsense!" you would ruin it. When reading a story, we intentionally set aside such questions in a process known as the 'willing suspension of disbelief', and this is what makes truly great stories come alive. Such an attitude was embodied when JRR Tolkien, author of The Lord Of The Rings was once asked whether or not Middle Earth was real. He simply replied, "*One hopes.*"

Now I'm not suggesting that this story is fiction at all; I wholeheartedly believe that the following story is in fact true. But I am also aware that most of you will struggle with that idea, it being totally foreign to the average Christian today, and that the journey towards actually believing it will take longer than this chapter. So if necessary, treat it as a work of fiction. Give me just a few moments of willing suspension of disbelief, and imagine what a wonderful world it would be if these promises really were fulfilled before Christ returns. Dream of a world where the Second Coming is not the evacuation of a bedraggled, surrounded platoon of believers, but the culmination of Christ's reign on earth, and the final, earthly coronation after a comprehensive victory. Picture how glorious the future of the church would be if this perspective were true. Allow yourself to wish that it might be the case. Allow yourself, when asked if you think this perspective is true, to at least say, "One hopes." Then see from Scripture that it is.[222]

About Christ and His enemies

The first time the gospel is preached in Scripture, it is God Himself who preaches it. Right after the fall of man into sin, when the Serpent successfully tempted Adam and Eve to eat the fruit of the Tree, just as the curse was being pronounced on man, woman, and the very ground itself, God promised that this anathematised state would not be permanent. Speaking to the Serpent, God says,

> "I will put enmity between you and the woman, and between your offspring and her offspring; he shall bruise your head, and you shall bruise his heel."
>
> (Genesis 3:15)

What is the content of God's gospel? Firstly, that someone will come who is the offspring, or literally the seed, of the woman. Throughout Scripture people are described as 'son of' and then their father's name is given. But Jesus Christ, in the virgin birth, was born without an earthly father yet with an earthly mother. He is the Offspring of the woman.

Secondly, God says that the coming Saviour would do battle with the Serpent. In this conflict, the Saviour be wounded in His heel by the snake, a painful but non-decisive strike, and at the same moment, the Serpent

---

[222] This idea about requesting willing suspension of disbelief comes from Doug Wilson, *Heaven Misplaced* (Canon Press, 2008) Introduction

would have its head bashed in. The Seed was coming to end the reign of the Serpent.

Anyone find it interesting that God frames His gospel in terms of a victorious battle? God's gospel is a gospel of winning. What is perhaps harder to explain is that Christians, who claim to believe this gospel of a one-sided, total victory, expect the influence of this gospel on our world to resemble total and utter defeat. We imagine our destiny is to lose here, badly, and we can only expect to rescue a handful of souls out of this world, rather than have any meaningful triumph in it. The content and the tone of God's message seem a far cry from what we usually expect lies ahead for the people of God.

The pushback to this might be that the promised victory lies in human hearts and a reconciling of individuals to a right relationship with God. Doubtless this is included here, and the relationship between God and man was almost irretrievably damaged by the fall into sin, and would have been destroyed forever if not for the work of Jesus. But if you read Genesis 3 as a whole, the context of this promise is not merely the damage of sin to personal relationships with God, but the damage of sin to creation in its entirety. Sure, central to that is God and man in perfect unity, but it also impacts work, childrearing, man's original commission to fill and subdue the earth, and even the ground itself. The coming of the Son was intended not merely to restore one of these things, but all of them.

Jesus' ministry reflected the kind of total warfare and all-encompassing victory that God Himself promised at the beginning. He defeated the devil at every turn, whether it was being tempted in the wilderness, in confrontations with terrified demons, and in healing the sick. His very miracles showed the extent of this takeover; a Christ who was only interested in human hearts and personal relationships with the Father would have no place for cleansing lepers, multiplying food, or commanding storms to cease. We know from His refusal to do spiritual tricks for the Pharisees that He did not do miracles to show off; He only did was essential to His mission. Clearly, this present world was very much part of that remit.

Jesus was explicit in His determination to destroy the enemy. In Luke 7, He tells us that:

"But if it is by the finger of God that I cast out demons, then the kingdom of God has come upon you. When a strong man, fully armed, guards his own palace, his goods are safe; but when one stronger than he attacks him and overcomes him, he takes away his armour in which he trusted and divides his spoil."

(Luke 7:20-22)

His own words tell us His intention: in casting out demons He demonstrated that He was stronger than Satan, and during His earthly ministry He was in the process of attacking him and taking away his stuff. Those of you who know the book of Revelation well will be aware that there is a passage that talks about the binding of Satan, preventing him from deceiving the nations. Many people place this binding at the second coming of Christ; but Jesus Himself says that this is what He was doing in His first coming. His time on earth was about ending the power of Satan.

There's plenty of biblical confirmation of this victorious warfare. Peter says in his sermon in Acts 10 that "...*God anointed Jesus of Nazareth with the Holy Spirit and with power. He went about doing good and healing all who were oppressed by the devil, for God was with him.*" Hebrews 2 tells us that, "*he himself likewise partook of the same things, that through death he might destroy the one who has the power of death, that is, the devil.*"

And it wasn't limited to Jesus. He passed this on to His followers, and we're told in Matthew 10 that He "*called to him his twelve disciples and gave them authority over unclean spirits, to cast them out, and to heal every disease and every affliction.*" Later in Luke 10, the seventy-two return rejoicing that the demons submit in His name, to which He says, "*I have given you authority to trample on snakes and scorpions and to overcome all the power of the enemy; nothing will harm you.*"

So Jesus' earthly ministry, and of course His death and resurrection, were in great measure about the destruction of the enemy. He passed on this demon-crushing power to His followers, and expected them to live out that same victory He had demonstrated.

Now at this point, I probably have everyone with me. Jesus came to destroy the enemy, and He did. But where we miss something is in how that applies to us today.

David Chilton in his book, 'Paradise Restored' makes the point that Scripture talks about the work of redemption in three stages: *Definitively*, *Progressively* and *Finally*.[223] For instance the Bible tells us that we have been saved (our spiritual rebirth by faith in Christ), we are being saved (our sanctification and perseverance in faith) and we will be saved (our glorified state at the

---

[223] David Chilton, Paradise Restored, page 34-35

Second Coming). Or that the kingdom of God has come (in Christ), is here (among God's people) and will come (upon His return). This is a clear and repeated pattern throughout the Bible.

All Christians believe in both the first and last victories of Christ, universally agreeing that He has won a definitive battle over Satan in His life, death and resurrection, and He will win the final victory over him on His return. But most Christians unfortunately think that there is no progressive victory between the two. In fact, they expect that any progressive victory will belong firmly to Satan, with the darkness getting darker and his influence growing before culminating in a satanic government right as Christ is about to return.

That is simply not what the Bible says. Scripture speaks of the progressive advance of the kingdom of God against the kingdom of darkness, and Christ Himself has promised that the enemy will not win. Before I get accused of imposing some external system on the Bible, let me prove it from the Scriptures.

Do you know what God's favourite Bible verse is? It sounds like a trick question, but it isn't. The most commonly quoted verse of the Old Testament by the New Testament authors is Psalm 110:1, which says the following: *"The Lord says to my Lord: "Sit at my right hand, until I make your enemies your footstool.""* This is the verse God uses most, and it is also one of the clearest verses about the progressive victory over Satan before Jesus' return.

So what does it mean? Well this is a Messianic Psalm, meaning it's about Jesus. It speaks of the Lord, that is, God the Father, saying to my Lord, God the Son, that He is to sit beside Him until His enemies are subdued. Pretty simple.

Here's a question though: When did this happen? That is, when did Jesus sit down at the right hand of the Father? Hopefully we all know the answer: it happened at the ascension of Jesus. *"But when Christ had offered for all time a single sacrifice for sins, he sat down at the right hand of God."* (Hebrews 10:12).

And how long will He stay seated there? Not until His enemies are victorious over God's people and on the verge of utterly destroying them, but until His enemies are defeated. Jesus will not stand up to return to earth until His enemies are placed under His feet. He will wait at the Father's right hand, not until the devil gains a near-total victory, but until the devil experiences a near-total loss.

Furthermore, we know that this verse is talking about prior to Christ's Second Coming, because of how the psalmist continues, saying in Psalm 110:2: *"The Lord sends forth from Zion your mighty sceptre. Rule in the midst of your enemies!"* Most perspectives tell us that when Christ rules the world in the future, His enemies will already have been disposed of, but this verse tells us that He rules in the midst of them. That is, His rule will be progressively established in a world that starts off opposed to it, and He will defeat those enemies one by one, not all at once. That is the progressive victory we spoke about, and says a whole lot about what we should experience this side of His return.

But it isn't just this Scripture that tells us about this progressive victory, it's all over the Bible. Genesis 49 tells us that He will rule until tribute comes to him from the peoples. Psalm 2 talks of Christ's reign in the nations, even as his enemies plot against Him, and they are ultimately defeated. John tells us that though we will have troubles in the world, that Christ has overcome the world, we have overcome the devil, and that our faith overcomes the world. Paul says that He currently gives us victory, and that we are more than conquerors, not merely that we will be one day. And he makes this absolutely explicit in 1 Corinthians 15, where we are told,

> *"Then comes the end, when he delivers the kingdom to God the Father after destroying every rule and every authority and power. For he must reign until he has put all his enemies under his feet. The last enemy to be destroyed is death."*
>
> (1 Corinthians 15:24-26)

We tend to think that Jesus will destroy every rule and authority and power at the end. Paul says that the end will not come until *after* they have been destroyed. Meaning that they are in the process of being destroyed now. We assume that He will return to put His enemies under His feet. But this passage says that He will reign, that is stay seated in glory, until that is the case. Meaning they are being put under His feet today. We tend to assume that death was the first enemy to be destroyed, in the resurrection. But it is not talking about His death, but ours. We will continue to die until every other enemy has been defeated, at which point Christ will return to end death, the final enemy. Though this foe won't be vanquished for us until His return, every other

It'll Be Class

enemy is to be destroyed through His church before the Second Coming.

Perhaps my favourite summary of all this is in Colossians 2:15, which says that Christ "... *disarmed the rulers and authorities and put them to open shame, by triumphing over them in him.*" This is a clear and direct allusion to a custom within the Roman army to bestow honour on generals who won the greatest victories in battle, known as a 'Triumph'. They would be invited to march through Rome, with all kinds of fanfare, pomp and glory, and with the disarmed, captive foreign military leaders bringing up the rear in chains, at the end of which these enemies would be executed.[224] It is this gruesome procession that Paul uses here in Colossians, and also in 2 Corinthians 2 for that matter, to characterise the total victory of Christ over Satan. At His first coming Jesus disarmed the enemy and took and his forces captive. At His Second Coming He will put them to death. What is happening today, in between those two events? His victory march.

All of this gives me hope for Northern Ireland. Whether they go by the name 'secularism', 'sectarianism', 'lukewarmth', 'liberalism' or anything else, there are plenty of spiritual enemies still lurking in our province. The kingdom of darkness seems to be taking ground, and the kingdom of God appears to be firmly in retreat. But this is a false dawn, a Battle of the Bulge, the final death throes of a crushed snake. All of these enemies will be defeated by Christ, through His church, *before* He comes back. Now, seeing as the current state of things doesn't look too pretty, we can say it

---

[224] https://www.britannica.com/topic/triumph-ancient-Roman-honour accessed 21st December 2021

would take a mighty move of God to accomplish such a turnaround. Great; then that's what will happen.

About the church

It should come as no surprise that the Jesus who came to fight His enemies and establish His dominion on earth sent His church to do the exact same thing.

Once again, this is not the common view of the church among most Christians today. The tendency is to view the church as a defeated force, an oppressed minority who must walk through constant exile without hope of success in this life. As famous Bible teacher, John Macarthur recently said, *"We don't win down here. We lose. Ready for that? ...They killed Jesus, they killed all the apostles, we're all going to be persecuted... We don't win; we lose on this battlefield."*[225]

Don't get me wrong; there is a price to be paid, suffering to experience, and a sense of enmity to be experienced as a Christian. We need to be prepared for this. That may well be our own experience. But is this kind of losing, this kind of defeatism, what Jesus commissioned His church to go and do? Or did He tell us we would go through such challenges in the way a wise general would prepare his troops for the suffering required in order to win a victory that is ultimately guaranteed? Might it be that there is a difference between losing one's comfort, possessions or life, and losing the battle?

I'll address two key texts about the church that give us the answer we need, the first of which is the first ever mention of the word church in the Bible, in Matthew 16.

---

[225] https://www.youtube.com/watch?v=Id-AXdKhzSc&t=626s accessed 21st December 2021

Most of you will know the passage; Jesus asks His disciples who people say He is, to which they reply that some say Elijah or Jeremiah or another prophet. Then He asks them, "And what about you guys, what do you reckon?" Simon Peter replies, "*You are the Christ, the Son of the Living God.*" Jesus exclaims in reply,

> "*Blessed are you, Simon Bar-Jonah! For flesh and blood has not revealed this to you, but my Father who is in heaven. And I tell you, you are Peter, and on this rock I will build my church, and the gates of hell shall not prevail against it.*"
>
> (Matthew 16:17-18)

There's a lot of potential content here, but two things that are of particular relevance for my argument. Firstly, though we all agree that there is a battle between hell and the church depicted here, it's essential to recognise that Jesus does not describe His church in a defensive position. Jesus does not say that the church is holed up, dug in, and needs to stand strong until the end, noble though that would be, and in certain contexts this may well depict the individual actions required of some believers.

Instead, Jesus uses the language of the 'gates of hell'. Now, I'm no military buff, but I'm pretty sure that gates are not offensive weapons. I have never seen a movie or read a book where an advancing army brings their gates onto the battlefield. As far as I know, gates are not used for flying over the enemy to drop bombs, they don't charge forwards on horseback, and they don't march through enemy territory. The Germans weren't in concrete bunkers on the beach on D-Day because thousands of Allied turnstiles and portcullises were sailing across the water to get them. Gates are for defence only.

Let's be clear: Jesus is saying that His church is an invading army. He is saying that we assault the gates of hell, behind which every dark spiritual force is hiding, desperate to get out alive. His church is sent not to merely hold ground or to wait things out, but to take back this world from the kingdom of darkness.

The second thing we are told is that we will actually succeed in doing this. How do we know this? Because Jesus says that these gates of hell will not prevail.

What exactly would it take for a gate to prevail? Well, it seems pretty simple: if you're attempting to batter down a gate, the gate prevails if it stays standing. In the context of a battle, a defensive gate would prevail if it was still there at the end. In the case of hell's defensive barriers, Jesus says that they won't remain standing once it's all said and done. We need to recognise this, because even many believers that have a firm grasp on the offensive mission of the church still have a belief that at the end of history things will look very much like that mission has failed. But Jesus promises that the 'ecclesia' - not He on His own, but He through His people - will succeed in tearing down hell's defences. At Christ's return the gates of Hades will lie smouldering on the ground and an open church door will have been erected in their place.

We may view ourselves as doomed to failure, and our experience in life may even reflect that at times. But from the perspective of the enemy, we are relentlessly advancing army hammering down the door, backed by the same overwhelming force that made demons scream in terror every time Jesus spoke a word.

The other passage on the church that needs addressing is the Great Commission, where Christ gives His people their marching orders. Matthew 28 records:

> "And Jesus came and said to them, "All authority in heaven and on earth has been given to me. Go therefore and make disciples of all nations, baptising them in the name of the Father and of the Son and of the Holy Spirit, teaching them to observe all that I have commanded you. And behold, I am with you always, to the end of the age."
> (Matthew 28:18-20)

Again, there is so much here that we couldn't possibly cover it all, but there are some essential highlights. Firstly, we are not told to go into all the world and make disciples. Or rather, we are not told to merely go and make disciples. We are told to 'Go therefore'. That is, we are to go in light of what Jesus said prior to telling us to go, which is that He has all authority on heaven and earth.

Now this may seem like a minor semantic difference, but it actually drastically impacts our perception of the mission. Most believers would agree that Jesus has all authority in heaven, but we imagine that we are going into the devil's world to try and rescue a handful of people out of it. That is not what we are told. We are told that Jesus reigns on earth now, today, this moment. We are not being sent to get people onto the last military transport plane out of Kabul before the Taliban starts public executions - *cough* thanks Biden *cough* - but we are here to announce that the regime has changed,

It'll Be Class

Jesus reigns, and all must submit to Him. The capital city has fallen, and we are emissaries to the outer regions of the empire announcing this good news. It's not that we're giving advanced notice of a reign that is on its way sometime down the road, but one which currently exists.

This ties in neatly with the second point, which is that we are to make disciples of all nations. Now, many Christians have rightly emphasised that this involves personal salvation and sanctification at its core, which it does and we all know that the private walks of believers and their public worship is a key part of this discipleship. However, we have often left it there, with the highest hope of most Christians being that we might succeed in discipling some people from within all nations. And that is insufficient.

Kenneth Gentry's excellent work 'The Greatness Of The Great Commission' outlines the distinction brilliantly. He explains that the Greek word for nations is 'ethne' - the plural of 'ethnos' - which has clear meaning, namely, *"collected masses of individuals united together by a common bond, as in a culture, society, or nation."*[226] If Jesus had wanted to limit the scope of this commandment to individuals, He would simply have said to make disciples of all men - anthropos - or if He wanted it to be solely political, he could have said disciples of all kingdoms - basileia.[227] But He didn't.

Instead He commanded His people to go and make disciples of entire cultures, the way entire nations and people groups interact, from top to bottom. We are not

---

[226] Kenneth Gentry, *The Greatness Of The Great Commission* (Institute For Christian Economics, 1990) page 51
[227] Gentry, *The Greatness Of The Great Commission*, page 53-54

commanded to make disciples *from* all nations, but *of* all nations. That is, the nation as a whole - the institutions, the media, the business, the education, the healthcare, the home life, the political systems, and the lives of individuals - all are to be completely Christianised. We are not sent to merely have some privatised piety and some nice Bible studies in the nations, though that is certainly part of it. But because Christ rules on earth now, it is important that His empire reflects His reign. He has *all* authority, so He wants *all* the globe to obey *all* that He commands. Jesus gathers twelve fishermen on top of a hill, and tells them, "That's my bit done. Now go take over the world." That is what we are sent to do.

There is much more we could say, for instance about how this must be achieved through the baptism and teaching of nations and is therefore a bottom-up, heart-outward process rather than a top-down, politically-driven one, or that this is a reinstatement of mankind's original mission to fill and subdue the earth, or what Christ means by all that He commands. But there is one more essential element of this commission that is of particular importance to us: it contains a promise.

At the end of His commission, Jesus says that He will be with us always even until the end of the age. Now what is the purpose of this promise? Is it merely a nice pat on the back, an emotional boost to send us on our way? Not at all. Rather, it was Him telling them that He is going to be intimately and personally involved in this process. He has not abandoned them, saying they should do this on their own. The King, who already defeated His Goliath, was going to work with the Israelite army to chase down and subdue the fleeing Philistine forces.

My question to us is this: do we think that the Jesus who succeeded in His incarnation, death and resurrection, is now going to fail in this task? Or will He succeed? Will the nations be discipled, and will it be as comprehensive and total as He commanded it to be? I believe it will. I'm convinced that we will a progressive recognition across the world of Christ as King, or as Isaiah says, "Of the increase of His government and of peace there will be no end." Believe your Christmas carols, people.

When Jesus said 'all nations' He most definitely included Northern Ireland. We've said that we have a Northern Irish culture. I believe that Jesus will succeed in discipling it, through His church, and that every last part of Ulster will one day submit to Him.

About the world

So if the enemy is to be progressively defeated before the coming of Christ, and if the nations of the world are to be increasingly successfully discipled before that time, then what will the impact on the world be? It's very simple: the world will be saved.

Now don't confuse what I'm saying with the heresy of universalism, which says that hell will be empty because everyone will ultimately be saved regardless of whether or not they trust in Jesus. There is no other Name by which men must be saved, and it is appointed to man once to die and after that comes judgement. You must believe in Jesus in this life to be saved, and many will not. End of discussion.

But still, the Bible makes repeated, marvellous promises about the salvation of the world which we will get into in just a tick. These have to be meaningful. The assumption of most Christians that a mere handful of people will be saved in an otherwise overwhelmingly unbelieving world does not do justice to what God has said will happen.

If universalism is not the answer, and neither is defeatism, then what is? Simple: it is that so many people will ultimately believe that we will be able to say that the world has been saved. In the same way that if there was a huge party with all your friends, co-workers, acquaintances and of course family present, and someone asked, "Who was there?" you could truthfully and meaningfully reply, "Oh, everybody." Or in a nation where a political party won a landslide election, the opposition not getting even a single seat in parliament, you could say, "Everyone voted for so and so." I believe in future generations, people will say of our province, "Oh, everyone there is a Christian." And it won't just be our province, but every nation in the world. Even England. This could not be said if a mere 10-15% of the population was saved, or even a cheerful 30-40%, but what about 75-80%? Maybe even 90%? I believe the future of the world looks a lot more like that.

So, anyone fancy getting hit in the face with a firehose of Scriptures where God breathes life into the future of mankind? Great, cause that's what you're getting.

Firstly, off the bat, Abraham is promised repeatedly that the nations will be saved. Genesis 12:3, the end of Abraham's calling, emphatically declares, *"all peoples on earth will be blessed through you."* This very concept, with almost the exact same wording, is said again of

Abraham by God in Genesis 18, then to Abraham after he is tested by God in Genesis 23. God makes this exact promise again to Isaac in Genesis 26:4, and to Jacob in Genesis 28:14.

The Psalms, and the Messianic ones in particular, are a rich source of confidence for those hoping for world salvation. Psalm 2, which we have already mentioned about the reign of Christ, includes a stanza where the Father speaks to the Son, saying, *"The Lord said to me, "You are my Son; today I have begotten you. Ask of me, and I will make the nations your heritage, and the ends of the earth your possession."* Here's a question on this passage which I heard posed by Arizona pastor Jeff Durbin: Do you think Jesus forgot to ask?

At the end of Psalm 22, which some of you will recognise as being a psalm about the suffering of the Messiah, the one of *'My God, My God, why have you forsaken me?'* fame, there is another powerful promise of world salvation. Verses 27-29 declare:

> *"All the ends of the earth shall remember and turn to the Lord, and all the families of the nations shall worship before you. For kingship belongs to the Lord, and he rules over the nations. All the prosperous of the earth eat and worship; before him shall bow all who go down to the dust, even the one who could not keep himself alive."*
>
> (Psalm 22:27-29)

Two words. Global. Salvation.

Let me blast through some more. Psalm 47 continues this confidence, saying, *"The nobles of the nations assemble* as the people of the God of Abraham, for the kings of the earth belong to God; he is greatly exalted." That is: all the heads of state will be believers. Sounds good to me. Psalm 64:9 says, "All mankind will fear; they will proclaim the works of God and ponder what he has done." Psalm 67:7 says, "God will bless us, and all the ends of the earth will fear him." Psalm 102:15 continues, "The nations will fear the name of the LORD, all the kings of the earth will revere your glory."

Psalm 72 may be the best of the lot, glorifying Christ throughout, and saying,

"May he rule from sea to sea and from the River to the ends of the earth. May the desert tribes bow before him and his enemies lick the dust. May the kings of Tarshish and of distant shores bring tribute to him. May the kings of Sheba and Seba present him gifts. May all kings bow down to him and all nations serve him."

(Psalm 72:8-11)

The prophets are not short on this either. Isaiah 2 declares,

"Many peoples will come and say, 'Come, let us go up to the mountain of the Lord, to the temple of the God of Jacob. He will teach us his ways, so that we may walk in his paths."

(Isaiah 2:3)

In chapter 65, Isaiah speaks of a great and glorious future time, with prosperity, peace, universal worship and the wolf and lamb lying down together. Most do not dare put this anywhere other than in the future age after the return of Christ. But look, verse 20 says, that *"the one who dies at a hundred will be thought a mere child; the one who fails to reach a hundred will be considered accursed."* In this Elysian age people will live long, but not forever. Death will still be a thing. It will be wonderful, but it will not be utopia. This marvellous period must occur prior to the Second Coming.

There are so many more. Isaiah 66 says that people from all nations will come to the holy mountain. Jeremiah 3 exclaims that all nations will gather in Jerusalem to honour the name of the LORD. Daniel 7 says that all nations and peoples of every language will worship Him. Zephaniah shouts that the nations on every shore will worship him, every one in its own land. Habakkuk prophesies that the earth will be filled with the knowledge of the glory of the LORD as the waters cover the sea. Paul in Romans 11 says that the Gentiles will be saved in such number that it will make the Jews jealous, and then all Israel will be saved. Later on in Romans 15, Paul justifies his entire ministry based on the multiple promises that all the Gentiles will be saved. Scripture goes on and on and on and on about the salvation of the whole world, it is positively giddy about it. And naturally I've only scratched the surface with my references here.

There have been multiple charismatic figures who have stood boldly prophesying that there will be a *'billion-soul harvest'* coming before the return of Christ.[228] Now I admire anyone seeking to bring the gospel to the lost in great number, and applaud all great work in this direction. But, if the promises of God are anything to go

---

[228] https://www1.cbn.com/cbnnews/cwn/2018/april/a-billion-soul-harvest-the-end-times-ushering-in-historys-greatest-revival accessed 22nd December 2021
https://www.youtube.com/watch?v=W_quU-X_toQ accessed 22nd December 2021

by, and if Jesus were here today, anyone who thought that only a billion more souls would be saved before His coming would be publicly rebuked for their unbelief. Somehow the idea that the salvation of the world promised over and over again in Scripture, means that a small, dishevelled fraction from within each nation get airlifted to safety at the last minute before the fire and brimstone rains down doesn't feel like an appropriate fulfilment of the glorious promises the Father gave to His Son.

I know you might not yet believe that this future will actually happen, but do you hope? And if you hope something like that might happen for the whole world, can you also hope for it to happen in Northern Ireland?

But it's all gone Pete Tong

You might ask: if Christ's victory is so total, His church so victorious, and His salvation so global, then why are we seeing the opposite in our time? It seems that things are getting so much worse and the church is collapsing so substantially that surely we must be living in the kind of ruinous ending most of us have assumed will come.

Three quick responses for you. Firstly, this is exactly the sort of thing we should expect if victory is imminent. Remember, we serve a Jesus who, whilst hanging naked on a cross, the flesh on his back ripped off to the point of exposing bone, slowly suffocating to death in public like a common criminal outside the city walls, likely took a moment to say to Himself, "Great, I've got them right where I want them."

This is exactly how God wins. God used a decrepit old man with a barren wife to be the father of nations; He used a shepherd boy to slay a giant; and He used a dead man to give life to the world. If the idols of the Western world - the secularism, the sex-obsession, the rejection of God and love of self - are to be destroyed, then their destruction will look like the destruction of all other demonic forces. Namely, a short-lived apparent victory for Satan whilst the kingdom of God has a brief sojourn in a grave, then a cracked stone, a shaking of the earth, a second-ever first breath, and a cry of anguish among hell's high command. These idols will have their ability to reign put to the test, it will be terrible and distressing, but they will be found wanting before long. Herbert Schlossberg wrote, "*The Bible can be interpreted as a string of God's triumphs disguised as disasters.*"[229] Let's expect history to reflect that.

That doesn't mean we won't suffer in our day - we might. Believing in long-term victory for Christ and his people is not a get-out-of-jail-free card. Actually it's more likely to land you in jail because you'll go around telling the powers that be that they need to submit to Jesus, which goes down poorly. But it means that your jail sentence is working to save your own descendants, the jailers' too, rewrite the law, and tear down the jail. It might be painful, but trust me, it'll be worth it.

Secondly, Jesus Himself promises that His kingdom will be great and glorious, but also gradual. What was it he said again?

> "*He said therefore, "What is the kingdom of God like? And to what shall I compare it? It is like a grain of mustard seed that a man took and sowed in his garden, and it grew and*

---

[229] Herbert Schlossberg, *Idols for Destruction*, p. 304)

became a tree, and the birds of the air made nests in its branches." And again he said, "To what shall I compare the kingdom of God? It is like leaven that a woman took and hid in three measures of flour, until it was all leavened."
(Luke 13:18-21)

The kingdom will grow to the point of being the largest shrub and of leavening the whole lump, but it starts small and gets there slowly. Jesus promised guaranteed victory, but He did not promise instant victory. In fact, He goes so far as to promises it will take a while.

We see repeatedly in Scripture that God's promises are simultaneously much bigger than anyone imagined, but also take much longer than they thought it would. When He said that the woman's offspring would defeat the Serpent, they probably assumed it'd be her first son. It took a few millennia. But He didn't just defeat the snake, He undid the curse. He told Abraham He would be father of many nations, then gave him one kid. But the Son of God also came through his lineage. It's slow, but it's huge.

If the Bible is anything to go by, then we should expect that discipling the nations to the point that they reject the ideologies they are currently embracing might take some time, and have some bumps along the way. It might well be the case that we are closer to the early church than the return of Christ. Ever considered that option? The odd summer drought, the occasional cooling dough (which I think stops yeast being as effective as it should) might crop up - it's hardly a reason to say that the tree is dead or the yeast is useless. The kingdom of God is still an unstoppable force, and the kingdom of darkness is nothing remotely like an immovable object.

And thirdly and finally, let me ask this controversial question: is it really getting worse? Sure, the West is getting worse, Northern Ireland too, we've got some big issues - I've been pretty clear about that. But the world as a whole is being saved at a remarkable rate. In 1900, there were only nine million Christians in Africa. By 2000, that number was 380 million.[230] Similarly, in 1900 80% of the world's Christians lived in Europe or North America, but just one century later 60% of them now live in the global South.[231] In China, there were around one to four million Christians in 1949. Today, that number is estimated to be as high as 100 million.[232] The nation with the fastest growth of Christianity is Iran.[233] The fastest growing single congregation in the world is not in the US or Europe, but in Hyderabad, India. It only started in 2005 and has over 300,000 members today.[234]

I hear the sound of creaking gates. And they aren't ours.

---

[230] Lamin O. Sanneh, Joel A. Carpenter, *The Changing Face of Christianity: Africa, the West, and the World* (Oxford University Press, 2005) Preface
[231] Ibid, Preface
[232] https://www.ft.com/content/a6d2a690-6545-11e4-91b1-00144feabdc0 accessed 23rd December 2021
[233] https://www.thegospelcoalition.org/article/meet-the-worlds-fastest-growing-evangelical-movement/ accessed 23rd December 2021
[234] https://www.christianpost.com/voices/how-one-church-in-india-provided-more-than-3-million-meals-during-the-pandemic.html accessed 23rd December 2021
https://www.charismanews.com/opinion/in-the-line-of-fire/53786-7-lessons-from-the-world-s-fastest-growing-congregation accessed 23rd December 2021

Discussion Questions

1 – What has your view on the future of humanity, prior to the return of Jesus, been up until now, and how do the passages referenced in this chapter either challenge or confirm that perspective?

2 – If the church is going to succeed in its mission, how does that impact our perspective on prayer and evangelism?

3 – If the whole earth will be saved, what does that mean for periods of darkness and spiritual decline in certain societies in certain periods of history?

4 – What can we learn from those places in the world where Christianity is on the march?

CHAPTER 7
FOR GOD AND ULSTER, OUR TIME WILL COME
Or: A Vision For A Christian Province

Did you know that one of the worst things to happen to you financially is winning the lottery? I'm serious. Statistically speaking, 70% of lottery winners end up broke and a full third go on to declare bankruptcy.[235] And it doesn't even take a long time: US lottery winners are more likely to declare bankruptcy than the average American within three to five years.[236]

Why do you think that is? Is it because witches gather around that spinning ball machine thingy they use to pick winners and curse it? Is it the government's fault? Does God just hate people who make money that way?

No, none of the above. Sorry for my upcoming bluntness about this but it's true; the real answer is that lottery winners are thick. That's mean. Bad Jamie. Ok, let me qualify slightly: at least in the area of finance, though perhaps not in any other part of life, lottery winners are thick. That's because, get this, they play the lottery. In the UK, your chances of winning the lottery jackpot are 1 in 45 million, and if you play EuroMillions,

---
[235] https://www.lovemoney.com/gallerylist/64958/lottery-winners-who-won-millions-but-ended-up-with-nothing accessed 23rd December 2021
[236] https://www.cnbc.com/2017/08/25/heres-why-lottery-winners-go-broke.html accessed 23rd December 2021

those odds are 1 in 140 million.[237] According to Save The Student, you are *"five times more likely to be struck by lightning, 64 times more likely to be crushed by a meteorite, and 4,000 times more likely to win an Oscar"* than to win the lottery.[238] Playing the lottery is one of the worst financial decisions you can ever make, because you give regular payments that will statistically never pay off, and is most often played by those who can least afford to make such payments. They might as well take thousands of pounds of their own money in cash, set it on fire, and hope that someone walks past, sees it, and is impressed enough to buy them a tropical island.

And of course, winning the lottery doesn't make someone who is financially dumb into the prudent 'wise man' from the book of Proverbs. If anything it exacerbates the problem, because it says that reckless gambling is a great idea. Hence the eventual ruin and misery.

Why do you think we haven't had a revival in recent times in Northern Ireland, at least, not on the scale that we want and need? Perhaps it might be because we have absolutely no idea what we should do with it. Such a revival, not backed up by good stewardship, could be like a complete waster with a winning lottery ticket. It could actually lead the nation into a far worse state than at present. If you don't believe me, just check out what happened to the region known as the 'Burned-Over District' in New York state, a region hit by multiple apparent revivals in the early 1800s, but which is now one of the most ardently secular, hardest to reach

---

[237] https://metro.co.uk/2021/04/09/what-are-your-chances-of-winning-the-lottery-2-14377628/ accessed 23rd December 2021
[238] https://metro.co.uk/2021/04/09/what-are-your-chances-of-winning-the-lottery-2-14377628/ 23rd December 2021

portions of the entire US.[239] Just as God does not bless every individual who wants to get millions with said millions, He will not bless every church that simply wants revival with revival. There's too much chance they will blow it and make everything worse. To get what they desire from Him they must be, at least to some extent, ready.

Before embarking on this closing chapter, let me make a quick disclaimer. Most people fancy that they'd make a pretty good benevolent dictator. We wouldn't put it in those terms of course, that's much too vulgar, but admit it: at times, we all think if we were left in charge, we'd do a good job. I'd get rid of bus lanes for instance, particularly on the Newtownards Road, where some eejit decided that one of the main arterial routes into Belfast needed cut in half so six people dotted around an almost entirely empty Glider can get down it a fraction quicker every half hour. Apparently exponentially increasing congestion and travel time is good for climate change, or some nonsense.

But anyway, I don't want this chapter to be full of my sweeping pronouncements about what the future of Northern Ireland should look like, or every action the national church should take in that context. That would feel just a tad presumptuous. At the same time, this book wouldn't be complete if I didn't try and say, "I think it could look something like this." If part of our issue is that we are not quite ready for a revival, then surely it's worth giving some thoughts on how we should prepare ourselves.

So, instead of acting like the Chief Potentate Of Northern Irish Christendom, with every 'i' dotted and

---

[239] https://www.5minutesinchurchhistory.com/burned-over-district/ accessed 23rd December 2021

every 't' crossed by mine own hand, I want to simply give a sound biblical framework for what we should do in the build-up to, and aftermath of, God moving in our province. And alongside that, I'd like us to imagine how genuinely spectacular that could be. Deal? Deal.

The myth of a secular nation

The first thing to say is that we are absolutely, unapologetically attempting to turn Northern Ireland into a Christian nation. As discussed when talking about the Great Commission, we want the entire culture to be successfully discipled. That is, we want our people to be Christian people, our families to be Christian families, our schools to be Christian schools, our economy to be a Christian economy, our politics to be Christian politics, our businesses to be Christian businesses, our healthcare to be Christian healthcare, etc, so on, and so forth.

To the average reader in our day, this will sound like a radical thought, but it really isn't. Northern Ireland was founded as an explicitly Christian province in 1921, and I am simply saying that we should continue to be one. Furthermore, we should strive to do so much more consistently so than we did in our first century, something which will be a blessing to all our nation's inhabitants, Christian or otherwise. The secularists are the radicals, who openly seek to overthrow our historic roots and install a secular society in all of the above areas we want to Christianise, and said secularism is entirely out of keeping with Northern Ireland's origins and history. A Christian Ulster is actually the default setting.

Unfortunately, recognising that the church is supposed to build a Christian society is something that has dramatically fallen out of fashion in recent times. Perhaps this has been best summarised in Greg Boyd's 2005 book, 'The Myth Of A Christian Nation' in which he argues that the church is guilty of seeking *'power over'* the world, particularly political power, meanwhile the Kingdom of God is a *'power under'* kingdom, practising the submission exemplified in the cross.[240] He rejects the idea of taking back a nation for God, and says that the church has no business being involved in issues of national morality like abortion or homosexuality. Though he's writing to an American audience, this likely reflects the average stance of a large portion of evangelicals in Northern Ireland today.[241]

There are some valid critiques in his book, and there have been many issues in Western Christianity that he rightly points out. But he also makes a few key mistakes. Firstly, his rejection of power over anything is misguided, because though Jesus did submit to death, no one took His life from Him; He willingly laid it down. And correct me if I'm wrong, but I believe He rose again. Is that right? And He now has power over sin, death, hell, and all the nations of the world, correct? Boyd's position almost functions like a denial of the resurrection and ascension of Christ. Such a glorious ending to Jesus' earthly ministry is a demonstration that power is not evil in and of itself; if it was, Jesus would be the most evil being in the world. Though they people of God should not clamour for any power other than the power of God, if they are part of a nation which invites them to participate in political leadership, they should do so, and do so as Christians. Godly leaders will

---

[240] Gregory A. Boyd The Myth Of A Christian Nation (Zondervan, 2008)
[241] Read a brief, approving summary here - http://pneumareview.com/gregory-boyd-the-myth-of-a-christian-nation/ accessed 26th December 2021

shoulder the burden of serving their nation whether in government, media or business if needs be, not abandon the nation to worse leaders in the name of eschewing power.

Secondly, framing everything in the language of 'power' is intentionally distasteful to a modern audience. It's actually a fine word - we use it of God all the time - but our culture abhors it. What if he has used this term instead: 'influence'? Remember how Jesus said we are salt and light, or yeast that leavens the whole lump - should we really not influence the national morality our society? We shouldn't end human trafficking, child abuse or racist lynchings? Boyd argues that the desire for Christian nations led to slavery. He's wrong, slavery was ubiquitous throughout every single nation in history until people explicitly trying to make their nations more Christian decided to outlaw it for the first time anywhere on earth. The original problem was not too much effort to be a Christian nation, but too little. Were these emancipationists examples of hypocritical, self-righteous use of 'power over' the world, as he accuses the church of using in other contexts? Or is it only socially popular sins that we're not allowed to touch? If Boyd took the same stance in the 1700-1800s, he would have found himself standing firmly alongside slave traders.

Thirdly, though he's right that simply seeking to implement Christianity by government edict is flawed, he wrongly imagines that we will be so ineffective in reaching the lost, that the only option for the church is to remain on the sidelines and whimper. What if everyone actually gets saved? Can the tens of thousands of Christian leaders, backed by millions of believing constituents, influence the nation then? Does Christianity have anything to say about what laws would be good or bad, like about not murdering or not stealing or anything? Or does the nation have to stay culturally Islamic, Communist or I dunno, Jedi, if that was the landscape when the gospel first arrived there? By Boyd's logic, even if Jesus saves almost an entire nation they are still not allowed to act like Christians in the public square. We wouldn't want the six remaining Vikings to have their raping and pillaging outlawed now, would we? You would?! You Christian nationalist! That would be an attempt to have *'power over'* the world, which is inherently sinful, according to Boyd. No matter how many personal lives and private homes Jesus rules over, we must never let Him out in public.

And finally, his greatest mistake is his unspoken assumption, shared by countless believers today, that a secular society is religiously neutral and therefore to be pursued by Christians.

This requires a bit of explanation, so you're getting a new paragraph. Perhaps a few paragraphs. Anyway, every single society, including its political system, is religious at its root. Each society makes ultimate judgements about the nature of life, meaning, value and purpose, and then builds its politics on that basis. The most basic laws - thou shalt not murder, for instance - are fundamentally religious. Why? Who says? Is human life innately valuable? Does that valuation only apply to humans, or also to wasps? What if a society decides that it is ok to murder Jews, or the Bourgeoisie, or the Tutsis, or black people, or white people? Is that wrong? These are not primarily political questions; they are religious questions with massive political implications. Whether a nation's laws reflect this or not - whether we have a

Nazi government, a Communist one, or a Western liberal one - they all make fundamental religious claims that shape society as a whole. Every single society in the world is a theocracy; it is impossible not to be. The question is not whether we will be a religious nation, but which religion we will serve.

Most Westerners assume that our secular societies successfully reached a point of religious neutrality not long ago. What we rather had is the latter ends of a Christian society, where the Christian morality that has infused the nation's consciousness, and even its subconsciousness, were enshrined in law and culture, maintaining an approximate moral status quo without the explicit mention of Christianity. So ingrained was this moral foundation that it worked not only when we kept silent about its Christian origin, but even as we outright repudiated it. Yet all the while, as we celebrated that the great driving force of secularism was advancing us further than ever before, we were entirely dependent on the momentum of fifteen centuries of Christian faith.

Unfortunately, the renunciation of Christianity was not without consequence. A civilisation cannot work feverishly to undermine the root of the moral and political laws that holds it together - that root for us being the authority of the Bible and its relevance to public life - whilst assuming that it can keep the society which had developed from such a source. That's like a group of men standing on a high branch merrily sawing away at the trunk just beneath their feet and praising the saw for its wonderful work of supporting them at such a lofty height. Then, just as the blade finally breaks through to the far side, delighting themselves in the marvellous, neutral state they have created. If everyone followed Boyd's ideas, apparently we should cheer every gash.

Inevitably, the trunk now sawn in two, the supposedly neutral state of the Western world took all of about ten seconds before gravity worked its magic and the thing began lurching wildly. In the last few years, in what should have come as a surprise to absolutely no one, the West has begun disposing of its alleged neutrality, and been busy installing a new set of gods over our social and political realm to fill the vacuum.

In certain systems, such a Communism and Fascism, the state itself fills the role of deity, existing for its own power and glory. However I would argue that our culture doesn't so much have the state for its god so much as we have inadvertently returned to an updated form of paganism. The Ancient Greeks would recognise our gods perfectly. If you took the world's first Grecian-Cockney, 'Arry Stotle, and brought him to our day, I dare say he would argue that we are ruled by a trinity of Eros, Eris and Narcissus. Eros was the god of passionate desire, and particularly of sex.[242] Eris, known to the Romans as Discordia, was not invited to a party with the other gods, and got revenge by dividing everyone into factions and setting them against one another.[243] Narcissus, the son of a river god, who rejected the love of a nymph and fell in love with his own reflection in the water.[244] To put them in today's terms, we are ruled by our sexual desires (Eros), supposedly victimised identity groups (Eris), and a love of self (Narcissus). It is these gods that now drive our legislation, our media and our culture as a whole.

---

[242] https://www.britannica.com/topic/Eros-Greek-god accessed 26th December 2021
[243] https://www.greekmythology.com/Other_Gods/Eris/eris.html accessed 26th December 2021
[244] https://www.britannica.com/topic/Narcissus-Greek-mythology accessed 26th December 2021

Of course we wouldn't't call them gods, per se, but they perform that role perfectly. It is against the idols of sexual freedom, victimised groups and self-identity that you are not allowed to blaspheme, lest you be called a 'bigot', a 'phobe' or a 'right-winger'. Cancel culture is nothing more than a 21st century version of excommunication. We teach the laws of these gods to our children, and want their gospel to fill our national psyche. Symbols of these gods - their flags, their holy days, their canonical books - are recognised by all. Businesses, public figures and social media must pay fealty to these deities. It is to these gods that we offer our children, whether it is in pre-natal sacrifice, or to be discipled by their bishops through our schools and media programming, or by simply not having any lest they should interfere with our lifestyles of self-and-sex-worship.

And of course, because every society is a theocracy, the state now backs these gods with its power. If you think this is an overstatement, 'Bill C4' was recently passed in Canada. This law explicitly forbids saying that heterosexuality is a human norm, or that anyone who either experiences sexual desire that falls outside of heterosexuality or a sense that their gender does not line up with their biology should or can go against this. It also outlaws any support for those struggling unwanted sexual desires to overcome their desires. It is therefore illegal to preach Romans 1, Genesis 1, or 1 Corinthians 6, the latter of which lists such sexual sins and then says, *"And such were some of you. But you were washed, you were sanctified, you were justified in the name of the Lord Jesus Christ and by the Spirit of our God."*[245] Preach that and

---

[245] 1 Corinthians 6:11

you'll get five years in jail. As apologist Joe Boot notes, *"This was not an anti-conversion-therapy bill, it was an anti-conversion bill."*[246] It passed through the Canadian parliament, without a single dissenting vote, to the sound thunderous applause. And such legislation is currently under consideration in the rest of the Western world as we speak.[247]

This, of course, must be undone by the power of the gospel. Just as a revival in an Islamic nation would lead to the overthrow of the rule of Allah not only in human hearts but ultimately in the public sphere, so a revival in our secular culture will end the rule of our 'secular' gods in private and in public. If we get the move of God we seek in Northern Ireland, it will move us in the direction of becoming a truly Christian nation.

Protestants, Catholics and Christendom

This total salvation of Northern Ireland in every aspect also provides us with a wonderful solution to the Catholic-Protestant enmity in our province. We have been taught to think that the apparently religious conflict in our nation's history was due to an overabundance of Christianity, and the solution would therefore be to decrease the province's religiosity. The evidence for such a supposition simply isn't there - secularism, despite only really being a governmental force from the time of Karl Marx, has killed far more people than any religion ever has, and in far less time. Hitler, Lenin, Stalin, Mao and the Kim dynasty have revealed big secular governments to be a far worse

---
[246] https://www.ezrainstitute.ca/resource-library/podcast/and-such-were-some-of-you/ accessed 26th December 2021
[247] Ibid

threat to human life and wellbeing. Furthermore Northern Ireland's violent history, like the history of slavery in the British Empire, did not stem from too much Christianity, but too little.

When it comes to resolving the divide, I don't mean both sides should embrace some sort of squishy ecumenism, pretending that our theological difference is unimportant. To do so would actually be to embrace a new religion, Pluralism, or as I call it 'Whatever Bro', in exchange for Protestantism and Catholicism. As Pluralism aligns perfectly with Secularism, it provides no defence for Christianity or Northern Irish culture and does nothing for the saving of souls or the province.

Wouldn't it be wonderful, rather, if Protestants and Catholics sought to demonstrate the truth of their respective positions, opposed though they may be on central elements of the faith, through teaching, sacrificial love for, and good works towards those who disagree? We agree that the Bible says that love for neighbour is the second greatest commandment. According to Scripture there is a common moral obligation on both sides. What if our society looked like us constantly attempting to outdo one another in that regard?

Speaking as a Protestant, it would be marvellous if Protestants actively moved into Catholic areas to be near to those they seek to reach, and served their communities with joy. It would be glorious if, rather than contentious marches in honour of past battles, we went around preaching the gospel in honour of the one battle that really mattered in which our King was utterly victorious. What if we went and learned the Irish language, and used it to communicate the good news of salvation by grace alone, through faith alone, in Christ alone, according to Scripture alone, to the glory of God alone? What if Catholics found themselves warmly welcomed into Protestant homes, churches and communities, not because we agree, but precisely because we do not and would like to persuade them? What if our hearts were broken for those who don't see the glorious truth we see, and we spent our nights in prayer that their eyes would be opened? Would that not be a glorious, truly Christian society? The revival we seek would produce that kind of nation.

And if our Catholic friends were inspired to do the same in reverse, we could have the greatest love-in of any country in the world, all without pretending we agree or that our disagreement is unimportant. Rather, the reality and the importance of our disagreement is what makes our kindness all the more essential.

One of the benefits of clarity on the nature and level of disagreement is that you can then go on to acknowledge and cooperate on the areas of agreement without worrying that you'll compromise on something essential. Protestants and Catholics both agree that God's word gives us the moral standard for all mankind, and it would therefore be entirely possible for devout adherents on both sides to work together to set up a Christian system of culture, business and government without compromising on their gospel beliefs. Douglas Wilson has called this kind of society, 'Mere Christendom'.

There is no chance in a small portion of a chapter in a short book could outline everything this society would consist of, but there are a few major fundamentals. This society would have a high degree of religious freedom for believers and non-believers alike, Christians being fully aware that saving faith cannot be forced, and if it could, it would not the prerogative of government to do so. Furthermore, it would place immense value on human life, seeing every individual regardless of background, skin colour, social status or class as marked by the fingerprints of God from conception to death. Abortion, euthanasia, paramilitary activity and unjust wars would be completely forbidden. Thirdly, in this nation the self-evident truths about the world as God made it would be honoured and protected. The fact that every child has a biological mother and father and that this is the natural human family would be seen not as some antiquated bigotry, but the essential building block of society. The belief that human emotions trump logic, reason and science, not to mention Scripture, would be disregarded. Finally, people would recognise that the primary responsibility for society does not lie with remote government bodies, but with individual people. We would stop asking our politicians to 'do something' about every minor inconvenience and social ill, and rather demand that they get out of the way so that we can take personal responsibility for the problems we see. Jesus told us to feed the hungry and clothe the naked, not to vote so that government officials would take money from our neighbours to do so.

A Christian nation is one which creates space for real worship of God without forcing it, honours human life at every stage, thinks clearly about the world as it really is, and takes personal responsibility to live well in it. It hardly sounds like the nightmarish hellscape many make it out to be. Actually it sounds flippin' great. With the surrounding world turning increasingly hostile to both Protestantism and Catholicism, there is a space and a need for us to work together for such a Christian nation in Northern Ireland.

To do this, the first thing that must happen is that Protestants must abandon Unionism, and Catholics must abandon Nationalism. Think about it: Protestants originally wanted to be part of the United Kingdom because it provided some protections for Protestantism., and likewise Catholics wanted to be part of the Republic of Ireland because it provided protections for Catholicism. That's where the Protestant-Unionist, Catholic-Nationalist alignment came from. Yet today, neither the UK nor the Republic of Ireland offer anything of protection to either. In fact it's very much the opposite; they are both secular nations that want to limit religious freedoms, and impose postmodern morality on the people of Northern Ireland from outside, Catholic, Protestant or otherwise. Assuming that a move of God here is not reflected in the UK or the Republic at the same time or in advance of a move here, that's unlikely to change. What benefit is there to actual Protestants or actual Catholics to have further integration with either? In today's world, connecting affiliation with these nations with a Christian denomination is no more logical than Protestants wanting to be led by an Ayatollah, or Catholics inviting a self-proclaimed Caliph to be their head of state.

My stance is more of 'a pox on both your houses'. Or rather, to be more precise, 'there's a pox already in both your houses, so we think we'll step outside for a bit so as to not die of the pox, thank you very much'. The determined march of secularism across the Western World means that places where Christianity is tolerated are becoming few and far between. Our aim should be to ensure that Northern Ireland is one of those places. At some point down the road, Protestants and Catholics need to have a huge argument with each other, preferably a civil one, about which kind of Christianity is true, and what that means, but I think we could unite today in saying that we would both rather have that argument somewhere other than a secular gulag. (The gulag will likely be named something like 'The Love And Tolerance Re-education Centre', but it'll be a gulag nonetheless.) Let's have our disagreement in a nation that actually permits both sides to live as free and full citizens, and work together to that end. Seeing as neither the UK nor Ireland look like they're going to offer this long-term, we should at the very least consider seeking our own nationhood.

(To be clear about what I am *not* saying, though I may tease the English - sarcasm is my love language - there's no space to despise them at all. We're not the SNP. Nor should we hate the Irish for that matter. On the contrary, my position is actually the best way to save them. But more on that in a bit.)

Fortunately, seeing as there is a common culture in Northern Ireland, one which is markedly different from either the UK or the Republic at present, we have a head-start in forming a legitimate nation state. Remember, we are a people who love our religious heritage, our families and our local communities - if we could only recognise how truly remarkable that is, it would be obvious that there are few better reasons for seeking to become a nation, especially when the surrounding world despises those things. Furthermore unlike the totalitarian secularism at work to the East and to the South, such a nation would be far more in keeping with what Northern Ireland was founded to be, and our historical culture both before and after that time. It would even be more aligned with Britain and Ireland as they once were. With those societies currently eliminating every last vestige of their distinctiveness, Northern Ireland therefore would not only be an essential keeper of Christian faith, but also the final conserver of both true Britishness and true Irishness.

Of course, the argument will come back that we wouldn't survive financially. That's true, not at the moment anyway. However, if we had a spiritual awakening that then encouraged the nation to look to Scripture in all areas of life, it would inevitably shape our economy, turning us into the hub of innovation, excellence and business that Christian nations are supposed to be, and we would thrive. During late 1800s, just after the 1859 revival, Belfast became a world-class industrial city with a thriving port, the centre of linen production for the entire planet, and the leader in world trade, not to mention having the world's largest tea machinery, fan-making works and handkerchief factory.[248] Almost all of the most prosperous nations in the world, according to GDP per capita, are smaller ones; why should we not be able to do the same?[249]

What's remarkable about this Mere Christendom option is that it's close to achievable. As mentioned in an earlier chapter, 40% of our population are regular church attenders, which is unusually high for the West. If we could find a way to get on the same side rather than fighting each other, we could move our province in this general direction right now. If such cooperation

---

[248] Dr. Jonathan Bardon (2006). *A Short History of Ireland*. Episode 41. BBC Audio
[249] https://en.wikipedia.org/wiki/List_of_countries_by_GDP_(PPP)_per_capita accessed 28th December 2021

could already bring us to the brink of becoming a Christian nation, then a great revival with another enormous swathe of the province coming to saving faith would certainly knock us over the edge. Only it's a good edge in this instance. A couple of hundred thousand conversions in the UK would barely be a drop in the ocean; in Northern Ireland, it would transfigure the nation.

Church alive

This may all sound like a grandiose plan far too complex for any single pastor, congregation or political figure to carry out. We want a nation that reflects Christ's rule in every single area, top to bottom and side to side, and yet we want it without an authoritarian centralised regime to drive it. How can that possibly be done?

Thankfully God has given us the plan for all this. It is not one individual or one congregation that will accomplish this, but thousands, and it is not the rule of a regime that will bring this about, but the rule of God's word. As the church across our nation uses the single offensive weapon we have been given, the sword of the Spirit which is the Word of God, this change will occur. It starts with the saving of souls - rebirth in the hearts of individual people - but goes on to transform their minds and their actions, and then as they live accordingly transforms their homes, before this redemptive power impacts the institutions of society of which they are a part, the governmental systems and the cultural forces in their nation. We are not speaking of a top-down movement, or neither really of a bottom-up one, but rather an inside-out one. Whoever is saved must live accordingly in every area of life, and thereby transform the world. Boyd's idea of 'power over' and 'power under' is a false dichotomy; the word of God will rather have 'power through' all portions of society as it saves, sanctifies and sends person after person to spread the rule of Christ wherever they go.

Perhaps you're like I was in times past, when I was tempted to find the notion of simply sticking to preaching the gospel to be a somewhat underwhelming answer to the problems of mankind. Is simply telling people 'Ye must be born again' the whole job? Perhaps substituting 'you' in for 'ye', but not much more? If that were the case, we could rent some billboards, boost a Facebook post and send carrier pigeons to every home with that five-word message, and get it done in a weekend. Sweet.

Unfortunately, or rather, fortunately, preaching the gospel is infinitely more comprehensive than that. Make no mistake, being born again is an essential element of the gospel, but it is not the whole gospel. To only preach that, repeating it like a mantra as though it contained a magical power to do everything God wants to do in us, is to preach a narrow, truncated, incomplete message to the world. If this were the only thing needed, I'm quite sure God would not have given us the rest of the Bible. The recent decline of multiple evangelical organisations claiming to be 'gospel-centred' due to their failure dealing with social and cultural challenges is, in my opinion, because they wrongly believed that the gospel could be pruned back in this way. Furthermore, the willingness of Christians to hide behind seemingly spiritual statements and practices in the name of focusing on 'the main thing' is guilty of making the same mistake. The gospel contains rebirth but is not limited to it. It is a big gospel.

Perhaps we can summarise the gospel by saying that Jesus Christ died in our place, for our, sins, and then rose again on the third day. It is on that last element that I wish to focus, because it is the element that is most often overlooked in practice, and it is from this point that the gospel draws its bigness. The resurrection of Jesus that shows that Christ's work is not only about personal salvation, central though that is, but it also does something cosmic. It was only after the resurrection that Jesus said that He had all authority in heaven and on earth, because it was at this moment that He won a definitive victory over sin, death, hell and the curse. This moment worked redemption not just for our lives, but for the whole universe. Indeed, the earliest creed of the Christian church managed to capture the celestial vastness of this good news in three simple words - which were not simply 'Jesus is Saviour '- but 'Jesus is Lord'.[250]

Our gospel is centred on the fact that Jesus is in charge of everything. Not that He will be one day, but that He is today. He is not merely the Lord of personal piety, of individual salvation, or of His church, though He is most readily acknowledged there. But He is also the Lord of lords, the Lord of paupers, the Lord of Ulstermen and Irishmen, Lord of the English and the Scottish and Americans and Europeans and Africans and Australians, Lord of male and female. He is Lord of marriage, Lord of sex, Lord of birth, Lord of childrearing, Lord of friendship, Lord of growing old together and the Lord of dying well. He is Lord of

---

[250] 1 Corinthians 12:3
Also read more in Colin E. Gunton, *Exploring and Proclaiming the Apostles' Creed* (Bloomsbury Academic, 2004) page 58

business, Lord of homemaking, Lord of healthcare, Lord of media, Lord of politics, Lord of macroeconomics, Lord of music, Lord of the arts and Lord of gardening. He is Lord of food, Lord of drink, Lord of supply chains, Lord of central heating, Lord of construction, Lord of clothing and Lord of furniture. He is Lord of walking, Lord of horses, Lord of cars, Lord of trains, Lord of airplanes and Lord of space exploration. He is Lord of philosophy, Lord of history, Lord of geography, Lord of biology, Lord of chemistry, Lord of physics, Lord of Mathematics, Lord of the social sciences, Lord of the English language, Lord of the Irish Language and Lord of Ulster-Scots. He is Lord of every molecule in the entire universe, from the neutron bumping around in the farthest flung star in space, to the chemical reactions in the brains of lovers, to the sinews that make up the index fingers of rulers as they sign bills into law. The gospel is that all of this belongs to Christ.

Now that is a gospel weapon fit for purpose. That's a message that can disciple a nation.

You see, the outworking of such a gospel is not that Christians should have some private spiritual life, detached from the rest of the world with little to say as to how they must operate in it. Neither is it simply that they should go out into all the world and stay civilly compliant, being broadly nice to everyone they meet. Nor is it some merely political activity, as though we could establish the kingdom through a single democratic vote once every election cycle. Yes, it encompasses all of the above and influences all of the above - it's not as though we can be Christians without a devout personal faith, or as though we do not need to be kind, practical people in the world, or that we could somehow go into the public realm and detach ourselves from our core identity in Christ as some claim to do. But the gospel goes further than any of these concepts alone, or even all of them combined.

Instead of a restricted message, we have a gospel which declares that everything in the whole world rightfully belongs to Christ, must be brought under His reign, and which sends us as ambassadors of that reign into our spheres of influence to establish His kingdom there. It is in many ways a continuation of the call given to Adam to fill the earth and subdue it, given once again in the second Adam to His church. The full gospel looks at every area of life and says, what does the rule of Christ look like here? How can this part of the world be filled with Christ, and subdued by Christ? How does Jesus command me to pray on my own? How does He command me to act in church? How does He command me to run a company? How does He command me to rule in politics? How does He command me to act as a friend? How does He command me to spend my money and time? How does He command me to treat that minor temptation, that small sin, that individual thought floating through my head? The gospel is that everything, everywhere, in every way, must bow the knee to Him.

Seeing as this is what the full gospel message contains, it also defines what true evangelism looks like. We are not just bringing the world to our faith, but bringing our faith to the world. Every believer should be an evangelist, not only in telling people the bare facts of the gospel, but in advocating for and demonstrating the kingship of Jesus in everything in which we are involved. It means we all have an obligation to understand exactly what the Scriptures say about our specific areas of responsibility, and both live accordingly as well as openly advocate for it as the right course of action for the whole world in that area. In doing so, we are heralds of His past victory, His current reign, and His future coming.

Revelation 1:6 calls the people of God kings and priests, which tells us something further about what this looks like. Priests were to understand the law of God, minister God's goodness to people, and reject idolatry and sin. That is our job in society - we must know God's law and its application to all of life, we must demonstrate and reveal the goodness of God in those spheres in which we operate, and we must push back on the inevitable idols that will seek to encroach on Christ's reign wherever we find them. Kings, on the other hand, were leaders, as the people of God should be. We should be the foremost advocates of great ideas that align with God's word and God's world, and be the tip of the spear in launching great initiatives in every sphere of society, for the reign of Christ is total and His kingdom is without end.

If this is what the gospel is, and what preaching it looks like, then a revived church will reflect that. We do not need a church filled only with superstar preachers, though we do need superstar preachers. But we also need every gift, talent, burden, passion and skillset placed in the church, all submitted to Christ, all praying for His kingdom to come wherever they are, all witnessing to their worlds in every way they can. We are ministers of God in every area, priests and kings to the whole world, chaplains to the cosmos. A Northern Irish church that did this could not fail to see their nation become utterly Christian. And do so quickly.

A light to the nations

At the very beginning of this book, we said that every single generation requires a move of God, and that ours in particular needs something of the earth-shattering, hell-shaking, nation-defining power of the Spirit poured out that changes the whole province. Few people recognise just how in need of something like this we really are, and fewer still dare believe it really will happen. So I'll draw this book to a close with the following simple exhortation: why the heck not?

We Northern Irish love to be self-deprecating, and tied to this we have for some reason, over the last number of decades or so, developed a corporate habit of ruling ourselves out of doing or accomplishing much of any real scale. We pair this with a national tendency of tearing down anyone who talks a big talk and aims for the stars, something which is not merely a manifestation of Northern Irish banter, but also of Northern Irish envy. Because we think we cannot succeed, we also want others to fail.

In many ways it has become a self-fulfilling prophecy - our most talented individuals often move abroad pretty early in life, seeking opportunities and affirmation of their skillsets that cannot be found here. We have become oddly timid, assuming that our national destiny is to be the butt of a joke and an economic basket case for whichever regional power wants to pick up the tab. And no one dare try anything ambitious; people will laugh if you fail, and despise you if you succeed.

Such mocking defeatism must be driven out of our souls if we are to see God do the sort of things we need today. Why shouldn't God use us for something wonderful? Why would we not be a candidate for a national awakening? Why should this not spread to the rest of the West? We did it before. Twice. Why not again in our day?

Unlike our current attitude, the people of Ulster started off as giant killers. Fionn mac Cumhaill - known better as Finn MacCool - was the fearless warrior of Ulster mythology, and legend has it that he volunteered to protect the people of Ireland from the enormous and wicked fire-breathing being of Áillen. This creature would show up at the annual feast of Samhain, before lulling everyone to sleep with music and then destroying the island with flames from its mouth. MacCool, keeping his ear open for the first note of Áillen's harp, was ready. Managing to stay awake, he waited for the creature to open its mouth to draw breath, then leapt at the monster and thrust the spear down its throat. He saved the island and was appointed the leader of the mighty Fianna warrior clan.[251] The lesson of that story is that, sure, our wee country might not be the biggest, but don't mess with us; we're daring and deadly when we need to be.

The Northern Ireland I see is one that has regained its warrior spirit and God-fearing confidence, not simply because it has gone through some self-esteem training with a shrink to sort out its daddy issues, but because it has been filled with the Holy Spirit. It is a nation that has reclaimed its historic identity and its national purpose, and is once again determined to shine like a beacon on the edge of the Atlantic. It is not a nation that people stream away from, but one they stream towards, a hub

---

[251] https://irish-at-heart.com/blogs/news/the-legend-of-fionn-mac-cumhaill-and-the-burner-of-tara accessed 28th December 2021

of life, freedom, innovation and genuine love for one another. It is a nation full of families, full of children, full of laughter and full of friendship. It is a nation where the churches are strong, prayerful, bold and faithful, fearing God and nothing else. It is a nation that raises spiritual gladiators and sends them to slay giants.

I am convinced that Northern Ireland is both a feasible and strategic location from which to recapture the West, or at least considerable portions of it, for Christ. Unlike the rest of the UK and most of Western Europe today, Northern Ireland is not too far gone. We have not fully given in to the secular dark age and its ideology, and the existence of thriving, bold, outreaching churches that believe and preach the Bible is actually possible here. There are also believers who have an interest in doing so. Plus, it's our Christian heritage. I don't know if you believe in spiritual wells that can be re-dug - I'm not sure if I do for that matter - but if they can be, there's one here. Maybe this island, as it has been before, will be the place to which believers flock, where they can be trained and equipped, and commissioned to bring the good news of salvation to the wider world once again.

We need a move of God to get us even close to ready for that kind of mission though. The Northern Irish people of God must kneel in prayer, and then stand firm. And heaven must back them up with the kind of almighty power that no mortal could either imitate or deny.

But it can happen here. It should happen here. It must happen here. I'll ask again. Why not?

Discussion Questions

1 – Have you believed that Christians should aim for a neutral society? If so, in what ways has this chapter challenged that perspective, and what does that mean for your life?

2 – If Christians abandon a sphere of society – for instance: politics, education, media or business – what does that mean for the society and the church?

3 – How does the idea that everything is to be brought under the Lordship of Jesus impact your daily life? Think about various areas: your home life, your work life, your relationships, your personal devotions, and everything in between.

4 – Northern Ireland will both experience and be used in a mighty revival. Seeing as that's the case are you going to do differently?

BIBLIOGRAPHY

I really couldn't be bothered finding out what the publishing houses, printing dates and edition numbers of each of the books on here are. Seriously, what on earth is the point of all that? If you want to know more about any of the books, you'll just Google them like a normal person, and all that information will be readily available there. I'm giving authors and titles only. If this bothers you, please contact my publisher. As this is self-published, that would be me...

Also, I'll include that promised recommended eschatology reading list in here.

Randy Alcorn, Pro-Life Answers to Pro-Choice Arguments: Expanded and Updated

Scott Allen, Why Social Justice Is Not Biblical Justice: An Urgent Appeal to Fellow Christians in a Time of Social Crisis

Greg L Bahnsen, Always Ready: Directions for Defending the Faith

Greg L. Bahnsen, Against All Opposition: Defending The Christian Worldview

Joel R. Beeke, A Puritan Theology: Doctrine for Life

E Calvin Beisner, Social Justice vs Biblical Justice: How Good Intentions Undermine Justice and Gospel

Humberto Belli, Ronald H Nash, Beyond Liberation Theology

Darrell L. Bock et al, Three Views on the Millennium and Beyond (Counterpoints: Bible and Theology)

Reinhard Bonnie, Evangelism by Fire

Joseph Boot, The Mission of God: A Manifesto of Hope for Society

Gregory A. Boyd, Myth of a Christian Nation: How the Quest for Political Power Is Destroying the Church

Michael L. Brown, Can You be Gay and Christian?: Responding with Love and Truth to Questions About Homosexuality

Michael L. Brown, Revival or We Die: A Great Awakening Is Our Only Hope

Michael L. Brown, John Kilpatrick, The Fire That Never Sleeps: Keys to Sustaining Personal Revival

Callum G. Brown, The Death of Christian Britain: Understanding Secularisation 1800-2000

Junius Brutus, Vindiciae Contra Tyrannos: A Defense of Liberty Against Tyrants (Christian Heritage)

Thomas Cahill, How The Irish Saved Civilization: The Untold Story of Ireland's Heroic Role from the Fall of Rome to the Rise of Medieval Europe

Christopher Caldwell, The Age of Entitlement: America Since the Sixties

D.A Carson, Becoming Conversant with the Emerging Church: Understanding a Movement and Its Implications

D.A. Carson, The Intolerance Of Tolerance

D.A. Carson, Christ and Culture Revisited

D.A. Carson, John Woodbridge, Scripture And Truth

D.A. Carson, John Woodbridge, Hermeneutics, Authority And Canon

Matt Chandler, Take Heart: Christian Courage in the Age of Unbelief

Tim Chester, The Message Of Prayer

Guy Chevreau, Catch the Fire: Toronto Blessing - An Experience of Renewal and Revival

David Chilton, Paradise Restored: A Biblical Theology of Dominion

David Chilton, Productive Christians in an Age of Guilt Manipulators: A Biblical Response to Ronald J. Sider

Charles Colson, Kingdoms In Conflict

Harvie Conn, Eternal Word and Changing Worlds: Theology, Anthropology, and Mission in Trialogue

Jim Cymbala, Fresh Wind Fresh Fire

Arnold Dallimore, George Whitefield: The Life and Times of the Great Evangelist of the Eighteenth Century Revival, v.1

Arnold Dallimore, George Whitefield: The Life and Times of the Great Evangelist of the Eighteenth Century Revival, v.2

Kevin DeYoung, Ted Kluck, Why We're Not Emergent: By Two Guys Who Should Be

Gary DeMar, Restoring the Foundation of Civilization

Robin DiAngelo, White Fragility: Why It's So Hard for White People to Talk About Racism

Rod Dreher, Benedict Option, The A Strategy for Christians in a Post-Christian Nation

Rod Dreher, Live Not by Lies: A Manual for Christian Dissidents

Mark Driscoll, A Call to Resurgence: Will Christianity Have a Funeral or a Future by Mark Driscoll

Mark Driscoll, The Radical Reformission: Reaching Out without Selling Out

Reni Eddo-Lodge, Why I'm No Longer Talking To White People About Race

Jonathan Edwards, On Revival

Jonathan Edwards, Religious Affections

Charles G. Finney, Lectures on Revivals of Religion

Viktor E. Frankl, Man's Search For Meaning: The classic tribute to hope from the Holocaust

Dan O. Via, Robert A. J. Gagnon, Homosexuality and the Bible: Two Views

Kenneth L. Gentry, The Greatness of the Great Commission

Crawford Gribben, The Rise And Fall Of Christian Ireland

Douglas Groothuis, Truth decay: Defending Christianity Against the Challenges of Postmodernism

Nicky Gumbel, The Heart of Revival

Jonathan Haidt, The Righteous Mind: Why Good People Are Divided by Politics and Religion

David Haines, Andrew Fulford, Natural Law: A Brief Introduction and Biblical Defense (Davenant Guides Book 3)

Collin Hansen, Albert Mohler et al, Revisiting 'Faithful Presence': To Change the World Five Years Later

Yuval Noah Harari, 21 Lessons for the 21st Century

Steve Hill, Pursuit of Revival

E.D. Hirsch Jr, Cultural Literacy: What Every American Needs to Know

Selwyn Hughes, Revival: Times of Refreshing

James Davison Hunter, To Change the World: The Irony, Tragedy, and Possibility of Christianity in the Late Modern World

Eddie Hyatt, 2000 Years of Charismatic Christianity

Gary Johnson, Guy Waters, By Faith Alone: Answering the Challenges to the Doctrine of Justification

Timothy Keller, Center Church: Doing Balanced, Gospel-Centered Ministry in Your City

R.T. Kendall, Holy Fire: A Balanced, Biblical Look at the Holy Spirit's Work in Our Lives

Arnold Kling, The Three Languages of Politics: Talking Across the Political Divides

Abraham Kuyper, Lectures On Calvinism

George Eldon Ladd, The Gospel of the Kingdom: Scriptural Studies in the Kingdom of God

William Law, The Power Of The Spirit

C.S. Lewis, Mere Christianity

C.S. Lewis, God in the Dock: Essays on Theology and Ethics

C.S. Lewis, That Hideous Strength

C.S. Lewis, The Screwtape Letters

Ben Lindsay, We Need To Talk About Race: Understanding the Black Experience in White Majority Churches

Greg Lukianoff, Jonathan Haidt, The Coddling of the American Mind: How Good Intentions and Bad Ideas Are Setting Up a Generation for Failure

John MacArthur, The Gospel According to Jesus: What Is Authentic Faith?

Eric Mason, Woke Church

Abdu H. Murray, Saving Truth: Finding Meaning and Clarity in a Post-Truth World

Ronald H. Nash, Life's Ultimate Questions: An Introduction to Philosophy

Mark A. Noll, Turning Points: Decisive Moments in the History of Christianity

Mark A. Noll, Is the Reformation Over?: An Evangelical Assessment of Contemporary Roman Catholicism

J.I. Packer, Knowing God

J.I. Packer, God Has Spoken

David Pawson, When Jesus Returns

Gordon Pettie, Do It Again Lord

Helen Pluckrose, James Lindsay, Cynical Theories: How Activist Scholarship Made Everything about Race, Gender, and Identity—and Why This Harms Everybody

Thom Rainer, Surprising Insights From The Unchurched

Leonard Ravenhill, Why Revival Tarries

Philip Ryken, City on a Hill: Reclaiming the Biblical Pattern for the Church

J.C. Ryle, Holiness: For the Will of God Is Your Sanctification - 1 Thessalonians 4:3

Francis A. Schaeffer, True Spirituality

Francis A. Schaeffer, He Is There and He Is Not Silent

Francis A. Schaeffer, How Should We Then Live: The Rise and Decline of Western Thought and Culture

Francis A. Schaeffer, Christian Manifesto

Alvin Schmidt, How Christianity Changed The World

R. Scott Smith, Truth and the New Kind of Christian: The Emerging Effects of Postmodernism in the Church

Larry Sparks et al, Ask for the Rain: Receiving Your Inheritance of Revival & Outpouring

John Stott, Between Two Worlds: The Challenge of Preaching Today

Glenn S. Sunshine, Slaying Leviathan: Limited Government and Resistance in the Christian Tradition

Carl R. Trueman, The Rise and Triumph of the Modern Self: Cultural Amnesia, Expressive Individualism, and the Road to Sexual Revolution

Benjamin B. Warfield, The Inspiration and Authority of the Bible

William Webster, Salvation, The Bible And Roman Catholicism

David F Wells, The Courage to Be Protestant: Reformation Faith in Today's World

James White, The Roman Catholic Controversy

James R. White, Mary--Another Redeemer?

James R. White, Scripture Alone: Exploring the Bible's Accuracy, Authority and Authenticity

James R. White, Answers to Catholic Claims: A Discussion of Biblical Authority

C.R. Wiley, The Household and the War for the Cosmos

Douglas Wilson, A Justice Primer

Douglas Wilson, Rules For Reformers

Douglas Wilson, A Serrated Edge: A Brief Defense of Biblical Satire and Trinitarian Skylarking

Douglas Wilson, When the Man Comes Around: A Commentary on the Book of Revelation

Douglas Wilson, John Knox: Stalwart Courage

Douglas Wilson, Heaven Misplaced: Christ's Kingdom on Earth

N.D. Wilson, Notes from the Tilt-a-Whirl: Wide-Eyed Wonder in God's Spoken World

Ch.6 Recommended Reading

Joseph Boot, The Mission of God: A Manifesto of Hope for Society

David Chilton, Paradise Restored

Gary DeMar, Last Days Madness

Kenneth Gentry, The Greatness Of The Great Commission

Douglas Wilson, Heaven Misplaced: Christ's Kingdom on Earth

Douglas Wilson, When the Man Comes Around: A Commentary on the Book of Revelation

To submit complaints, hate mail, or any other form of communication, please check out the following website: **www.thecomingulsterrevival.com**. Ta!

Printed in Great Britain
by Amazon